Childminder's Guide to Play and Activities

Also available from Continuum

Behavioural, Emotional and Social Difficulties: A Guide for the Early Years, Janet Kay

Childminder's Handbook, Allison Lee

Co-ordinating Special Educational Needs: A Guide for the Early Years, Damien Fitzgerald

Good Practice in the Early Years, Janet Kay

Help Your Child with Literacy, Caroline Coxon

Help Your Child with Numeracy, Rosemary Russell

Medical Conditions: A Guide for the Early Years, Pam Dewis

Observing Children and Young People, Carole Sharman, Wendy Cross and Diana Vennis

Protecting Children, Janet Kay

Childminder's Guide to Play and Activities

Allison Lee

continuum

Continuum International Publishing Group

Continuum UK	Continuum US
The Tower Building	80 Maiden Lane
11 York Road	Suite 704
London SE1 7NX	New York, NY 10038

www.continuumbooks.com

British Library Cataloging-in-Publication Data
A catalogue record for this book is available from the British Library.

ISBN: 9780826494641 (paperback)

Library of Congress Cataloguing-in-Publication Data
Lee, Allison.
    Childminder's guide to play and activities / Allison Lee.
        p.   cm.
    Includes index.
    ISBN-13: 978-0-8264-9464-1 (pbk.)
    ISBN-10: 0-8264-9494-1 (pbk.)
1. Toddlers--Development. 2. Child development. 3. Early childhood education--
Activity programs. 4. Creative activities and seat work. 5. Play. I. Title.
    HQ774.5.L44 2007
    649' .51--dc22

                                                            2007017831

Typeset by Free Range Book Design & Production Limited
Printed and bound in Great Britain by Ashford Colour Press Ltd, Gosport, Hants.

Contents

vi Contents

viii Contents

Acknowledgements

I have enjoyed writing this book immensely but it would have been a very difficult project had it not been for the practical and moral support I have been shown by my colleagues, friends and family.

Special thanks go to the parents of the children I have had the pleasure of working with, both past and present, and especially to those who have given their consent for me to use pictures of their children within this book.

Finally, very special thanks to my husband Mark and sons Sam and David who have believed in me and supported me through the good times and bad!

I hope you, the readers, enjoy this book and find in useful in planning and providing activities for both your own children and those you care for.

This book is dedicated to Irene Parker, with love.

Preface

Providing good quality childcare is something that I have been passionate about for many years. I believe that every child should have the opportunity to explore, learn and develop in a stimulating environment with appropriate resources available.

All early years workers, including childminders and nannies, need to develop a good understanding of how a child plays in order to be able to plan and provide suitable activities.

This book will help you to:

- Understand the stages of child development from birth to 16 years.
- Plan and support children's learning and development.
- Provide suitable activities to promote each aspect of a child's development.
- Encourage respect and values in children.

Introduction

Children play every day, and through play they can learn about the world around them.

As well as being integral to early learning and educational development, it is important that childcare practitioners – including childminders and nannies – encourage the *right* to play, and through this promote all-round child development, including social, physical and emotional skills.

By carefully planning play and activities for your daily routine you can encourage children to explore, try out new experiences and ask questions. By introducing a wide range of craft materials and resources you will help children to develop creative skills, and an early introduction to exercise will encourage sensible habits for life.

This book has been written specifically for all home-based child carers who, unlike teachers, do not have the advantage of pooling their ideas and suggestions with colleagues. Childminders and nannies usually work alone and as such have only their own ideas to work with. This book will encourage home-based child carers to look at the way they plan for the needs of the children in their care – sometimes over a wide age range – and will help them to develop ideas suited to the learning and development of each individual child.

It is not always easy for individuals to reflect on the service they provide and, without the input of colleagues, activities and routines can become stale and ineffective. This book will encourage the reader to look at the importance of play and understand how it helps a child to develop.

Throughout, explanations and ideas are given to cover all the major areas of a child's learning and development. In addition, full information and support are given on

- The key stages of child development.
- The national curriculum, as background information on what is happening in schools. This will aid your planning of appropriate activities for the children in your care which take into account their stage of learning and the experiences they already have.
- Planning activities for children of different ages, so you can ensure that their needs as individuals are met.
- How you might go about encouraging respect and values in children (Chapter 11).
- How to promote safe play (Chapter 12).

In some of the chapters there are sections on how you can successfully incorporate Information and Communication Technology (ICT) into your planning of play and activities. ICT is ubiquitous in today's world of learning and play, and is used widely in schools (although it should not be allowed to take the place of traditional play).

What is Play?

What exactly does the word 'play' mean to you? There are in fact many meanings. Amusement, having fun, messing around, and relaxing are all words which are conjured up when thinking about the meaning of play.

All children have a fundamental right to play but, contrary to popular belief, children are not born with a natural instinct for playing; they do in fact *learn* how to play. A child learns how to play from a variety of sources and in a variety of ways. They learn from watching adults and other children and from repetition.

Play should be a valuable part of all of our lives but it is a *necessity* in the lives of children. When they play, children are in control, they are allowed to make mistakes, explore and experiment.

It is essential that you, the practitioner, understand the importance of play in order to fulfil a valuable role in helping and encouraging the child to get the most out of play. There is no age limit to the enjoyment of play and even the very youngest babies should be encouraged to learn about the world around them. A young baby's first 'toys' may be their fingers and toes. Exploration is a vital part of learning and it is worth remembering that a child learns more, and at a greater speed, during their pre-school years than at any other time in their lives. It goes without saying, then, that this time is extra special and should not be wasted. Children are inquisitive and ready to learn and it is up to you to nurture this inquisitiveness and encourage and stimulate the child.

Exercise

Think about what play means to you as an individual. Make a list of the ways in which babies, children and adults 'play' and why it is important for each to be allowed the opportunity to play.

How Play Assists Learning

Play is the main way in which children learn, and play can take many different forms and shapes. Figure 1 shows the areas in which children learn and develop while playing.

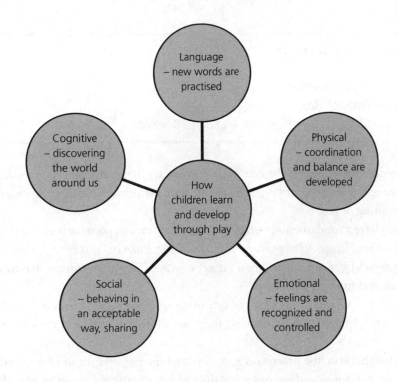

Figure 1.1 How children learn and develop through play

The Main Types of Play

There are four main types of play:

1 Solitary Play
2 Parallel Play
3 Associative Play
4 Cooperative Play

Solitary Play

This stage of play takes place from birth to around two years of age. During this time most children will play on their own. They will require help and encouragement from an adult but will spend most of their time exploring alone, watching and copying others. Although not old enough to play with other children at this stage, they will join in games with adults such as action rhymes and peek-a-boo.

> ### Exercise
> Observe a child below the age of two years while they are playing. Do they need an adult to be involved? How long is their attention span?

Parallel Play

From the age of two to three years, children become more aware of each other and will happily play 'alongside' another child. It is usual for children of this age to be unwilling to share or play happily *with* another child.

> ### Exercise
> Observe a group of children aged between two and three years of age whilst they are playing. How do they react to one another? Compare the way this age group of children play with that of children in the three- to four-year age bracket. How do they differ?

Associative Play

From the ages of three to four years, children will usually continue to play alongside one another rather than together, however they will now begin to take note of what others are doing and begin to copy other children.

Cooperative Play

This is the final stage of play and, again, takes place from the age of four and above. Many children of this age group will now have started attending playgroup or nursery school and they are at the age when they usually enjoy the company of other children of a similar age. They are learning to share and cooperate with each other.

> **Exercise**
>
> Observe how involved a group of children aged four and above become when playing. Watch how they use their imaginations and experiences to extend the activity. Note how much cooperation there is between the children and the 'rules' by which they play.

There are, of course, many kinds of play. Play can be noisy and boisterous or quiet and calming. It can be messy and creative or imaginative and emotional. Children can learn and have fun through spontaneous play in much the same way as they can through structured play.

Children should be encouraged to play with and without props, and both indoors and out. They should learn to play alone, with children or adults and with a combination of both.

Structured Play

This is when the play is planned by you, the adult. Structured play is particularly helpful if you are intending to help a child to learn or develop a particular skill, as you can 'structure' the activity around their particular developmental stage.

Free Play

This is when children are allowed to choose what they want to play. They are allowed the freedom of choice to play in an unplanned way.

> **Exercise**
>
> Watch the children whilst they are enjoying free play. Observe how they are playing and how they extend the activity in order to continue something they find enjoyable.

When a child is given the opportunity to play in an unstructured way where they can choose the type of play for themselves, they will draw on all their experiences as they take charge of the free play situation. If a child is playing at dressing-up or in the home corner they may draw on their happy, sad, painful or frightening experiences, and whilst the child should be allowed to take charge of the situation during free play opportunities, this does not mean that adults should not offer support and assistance when needed.

Childminders have the difficult job of learning how to enrich a child's play experiences without taking over the situation. For a child to understand the equal importance of both structured and free play the adults around them need to know how to support both types of play successfully. As a childminder you should be available to listen to the children, answer questions and offer suggestions during the time that children are enjoying free play.

Exercise

Make a list of five different activities which may be enjoyed for both structured and free play. How much adult input will be needed for each activity?

The Importance of Play in Helping a Child to Develop

Children develop at difference times and at different stages. No two children are alike and it is important not to make comparisons between children of a similar age. There are many characteristics which may affect a child's development, for example the number and age of their siblings, premature birth, diet and home life etc. Many parents become worried if their child is not walking or talking by a certain age, but although we may use certain milestones as an 'average' it really is not possible to pigeon-hole children's developmental stages.

There are five main areas of development associated with children and we shall take a look at these areas in detail now.

Social Development

Social development increases when a child is old enough to enjoy the company of other children. Although parents are in a unique position to help and encourage their children from a very young age, the real socializing comes about when a child is old enough to build relationships and friendships of their own. Children need to learn the importance of cooperation, sharing and taking turns. By setting good examples ourselves and encouraging children to take part in group activities we can help promote the importance of understanding the needs of others.

Emotional Development

It is important for children to explore their feelings and to be able to understand their own emotions. Children can often have very powerful emotions, and if they are not in control of these emotions, they can become frightened and insecure. By encouraging children to explore and understand their own feelings through play they will also learn to understand and respect the feelings of those around them and learn to build happy relationships with others. An emotionally stable child will become independent and feel confident and secure.

Communication and Language Development

It is often wrongly assumed that communication is all about speech. In fact there are many ways in which we can, and do, communicate with one another every day, and it is not all done verbally. Body language, facial expressions, gestures, signing, reading and writing are all part of a child's language development. Very young children and babies have the means of expressing themselves long before they learn the art of speech. Crying is of course a baby's primary method of communication, and they do this for a number of reasons: hunger, tiredness, discomfort, boredom, pain etc. It is often said that a child who experiences tantrums at the toddler stage is going through the 'terrible twos'. In my experience this stage is one of the most frustrating for a child. They have the desire to explore and need to express themselves, but often lack the maturity to do so successfully. A child of 14 months may become frustrated at not being able to walk, and likewise a child of 18 months may be unable to express verbally how they feel and this often results in a tantrum.

It is important that adults communicate regularly with children at all levels. Language development can be gained from a variety of sources, from everyday talking to reading stories, and encouraging children to ask and answer questions, singing and television are some of the sources of language which can help children to learn new words.

Intellectual Development

Intellectual development is the way in which a child responds to and thinks about the things around them. Concentration, memory and attention span are all aspects of intellectual development. Imagination plays a huge part in this area of a child's development and they should be encouraged to play in ways that help them to explore the world around them. Introducing colours and numbers into play will stimulate a child's intellect.

Physical Development

Physical development can be split into two categories: *fine motor skills* and *gross motor skills*.

Fine motor skills

This area of development covers activities which help with a child's dexterity and coordination. Using building blocks, playing with jigsaws and exploring with sand and water are all ways of developing a child's fine motor skills.

Gross motor skills

This area of development covers activities which promote a healthy lifestyle and exercise. Outdoor play, running, climbing, jumping, riding on bicycles etc., are all ways of providing children with fresh air and physical development.

Exercise

Make a list of materials and resources which you could provide to help a child to enjoy:
1. Social play
2. Emotional play
3. Communication and language play
4. Intellectual play
5. Physical play.

It is important for child carers to know the main stages of development in order to help and encourage a child and give them a good start in life.

There are many different ways of 'categorizing' a child's development. In addition to the five areas looked at above, it can be helpful to concentrate on the 'Seven Cs':

- Concentration
- Communication
- Competence
- Creativity
- Coordination
- Confidence
- Cooperation

In order to help and encourage a child to develop in these areas, it is important that we fully understand each category ourselves.

Concentration

This is an area which some children find very difficult. It is important to remember that each child is unique and an activity which one child finds stimulating may be completely boring to another. Children's attention spans vary enormously. Some children may be happy to sit and do a jigsaw for 15 minutes whereas another child may flit from one activity to another in the space of a very short time. Although it is important to encourage a child to persevere with an activity, you must also remember that learning and play should be fun and forcing a child to do something they are not enjoying or which they find boring may have an adverse effect on their development.

Although we all need to concentrate at some time, and it is important for children to learn the importance of concentration, it is vital that we recognize the differing needs and abilities of each child.

Communication

The rate at which children learn to talk varies enormously. Some children can speak clearly, stringing several words together, from the age of around eighteen months while others are still using unclear, single-word commands at the age of three years. It is, however, worth bearing in mind that early progress does not necessarily have any particular bearing on a child's later ability. Speech is one of the most important aspects of a child's development in the first three years of their life and other aspects of their development are dependent upon their ability to talk.

Competence

As a child becomes more confident in their own abilities they can be encouraged to stretch themselves further. Hopefully the activities you provide for the child will encourage them to learn and become better at the tasks with practice. Repetition is a good way of building a child's competence, and you should encourage children to develop their self-help skills as they become more competent.

Creativity

There are many areas in which children can express themselves creatively and they should be encouraged to do so using a variety of materials including, paint, play dough, clay, crayons, sand, water, glue and collage materials. Creative play is essential for a child to explore their senses and it is often easy to include ways of introducing sight, smell, touch, sound and taste into creative play.

Coordination

Coordination is covered in most things we do on a daily basis. Getting dressed, feeding and drinking all need this important skill. It is relatively simple to provide activities to cover coordination and you should look at ways to incorporate both fine and gross motor skills into the activities you provide. Young children may appear clumsy when they attempt an activity for the first few times but you will notice their skills improve as they learn to manipulate and improve their hand-eye coordination. Coordination is part of children's physical development and they must learn both fine and gross motor skills. Muscle development, strength and control will all be improved through activities aimed at coordination.

Confidence

It is important that the activities and experiences you provide are suitable for the age and ability of the child they are aimed at. A child will quickly lose interest and confidence when faced with a task which is either too easy for them or too difficult. Activities can and should be adapted as a child's ability progresses, but you will not increase their confidence by having unreasonable expectations of what they should achieve. It is important to remember that children should not be pushed into doing something they are not happy to do; although encouragement should be given, a child must be allowed to choose whether or not they wish to take part in a particular activity. Children often respond well to singing and dancing. However, a child who is new to a setting, who has perhaps just started playschool or nursery, may prefer to sit and watch for a while. Remember that not all children are destined to take centre stage, and whilst some children love performing others prefer to take a back seat.

Cooperation

This is a very important skill that all children must not only be encouraged to learn but should also be taught to understand its importance. There is little point in drumming into a child why they must learn to share and take turns, if you do not explain to them why this is so important. Children will develop strong friendships as they get older if they learn how to value others and understand the feelings and needs of those around them.

Child Development 0–16 Years

Chapter Outline

If you look at a baby of three months old and compare him or her with a child of three years, the differences will be obvious and striking. During the first few years of a child's life they grow and develop at a tremendous rate. The child goes from a tiny baby who is completely dependent on his or her carer for everything, to becoming an individual in their own right with likes and dislikes. They will be mobile, have the ability to communicate and be able to take part in the everyday tasks necessary for survival.

It is important to remember that while all children grow and develop at varying rates there are realistic expectations which should be considered. While it is vital that we do not underestimate children, we must not expect too much from them.

Child development is the growth of babies through childhood. Although all children will go through the same stages of development they will do so at differing speeds. Some children are confident walkers by the time they reach their first birthday, for example, whilst others may be nearer two years of age before taking their first tentative steps. Although the actual stages of development in terms of age differ enormously, what is clear is that a child must reach a certain degree of development in one area before they can successfully move on to the next stage. For example, a child will learn to sit before they can stand and to stand before they can walk etc.

It is therefore important to remember that although when speaking we often refer to the growth and development of the 'average' child, there is, in fact, no such thing and it is the child as a *whole* which we should be concerned with.

Stages of Development and Play

The speed at which a child reaches each stage of development will depend on many things, including whether they have any impairment or communication difficulties, together with their personal experiences. For example, a child from a large family will probably find it easier to mix with other children and play cooperatively than, say, a child who has no siblings and who may find making friends and settling into new environments more difficult. The chart below shows the different stages of play which children go through.

Age of Child	Stage of Development	Explanation
0–2 years	Solitary play	Most children of this age play alone.
2–3 years	Spectator play	Children enjoy watching what others are doing but rarely join in.
2–3 years	Parallel play	Children play alongside each other but rarely play together.
3–4 years	Associative play	Children are now beginning to form friendships. They have preferences and may occasionally play cooperatively.
4–5 years	Cooperative play	Children have now learned to play cooperatively and support one another.
5 years and over	Cooperative play	Children move on from simply playing to taking part in games with rules. These rules are very different as they are 'set' rather than made up as they go along.

Figure 2.1 Stages of play

Although all children grow and develop at different rates we will now look at the intervals of growth and development. It is important to remember that these intervals are only a rough guide; all children are unique and no two children will grow and develop at exactly the same rate.

Social Development

0–3 months
From birth to three months babies are very sociable beings. They enjoy the intimacy of caring routines such as feeding, cuddling and bathing. A distressed baby can often be easily soothed when they hear, see, smell or feel their main carer.

3–6 months
Babies of this age are very sociable and enjoy taking part in what is going on around them.

6–9 months
Between the ages of six and nine months babies are still very sociable. They enjoy company immensely and will often laugh along with others. They may begin to feed themselves with finger foods as their social skills begin to develop.

9–12 months
By the time a child reaches the age of nine to twelve months they will have discovered how to play alone and will not be as dependent on others for their entertainment. They will be able to entertain themselves for lengthy periods of time and will enjoy music and nursery rhymes.

1 year
A whole new world is opening up socially to a child of this age as they relish being mobile and discovering things for themselves. By now they will have developed a sense of identity which will increase as they get older and become more confident.

2 years
The confidence of the average two-year-old child will have soared as they become more and more independent. They will enjoy carrying out simple tasks and learning how to dress and feed themselves.

3 years
Socially a child will have come a long way by the time they reach their third birthday. They will now be capable of making friends, and although they may understand how to negotiate and take turns, they may well resort to tantrums and quarrels if they do not get their own way.

4 years
Children enjoy socializing and making friends at this age and should be encouraged whenever possible. Most children of this age will have started playgroup, nursery or even school and the scope for forging friendships will have increased dramatically.

5 years
By the time a child has reached their fifth birthday they will have made a number of friends. They will enjoy being with others and will have developed an awareness of their gender

and their own background and culture. This is the age when children begin to work out for themselves what is right and wrong and understand the importance of sharing and taking turns.

6–8 years

Between the ages of six and eight years some children become less sociable and prefer to spend increasing amounts of time alone, while others prefer to forge a 'special' friendship with just one 'best' friend.

8 years and over

Children fall in and out of friendships easily at this age as they change and develop themselves. While some children prefer to have one special friend, others prefer to surround themselves with a group of trusted companions. As the child's confidence grows they begin to find their own comfortable place in their social circle.

Emotional Development

0–3 months

At around 5–6 weeks babies first start to smile and between 3 and 6 weeks later they will be able to recognize the face and voice of their main carer.

3–6 months

Babies of this age are immensely trusting and enjoy the security they derive from being in contact with others and receiving attention from them.

6–9 months

Babies start to become wary of people they do not know and may become distressed if their mother or main carer goes out of their sight.

9–12 months

At this age babies enjoy being with people they are familiar with and may become increasingly distressed in the company of people they do not recognize.

1 year

By the time a child has reached his or her first birthday they have become aware of the moods of other people and will often react accordingly. They may imitate feelings of happiness or grief by copying the reactions of those around them.

2 years

Many children of around the age of two years become easily distressed about things they are unsure of or do not understand. For example, they may develop a fear of the dark or a phobia of dogs or spiders. The child's sense of identity progresses rapidly at this age and their memory increases.

3 years

Children of this age are becoming more and more aware of their own feelings and emotions and may well be able to describe how they are feeling and explain the reasons behind it. At around the age of three years children start to become aware of the variances in others and understand gender differences.

4 years

Children around four years are very similar emotionally to a three year old, although their imagination increases dramatically and they are capable of imagining a wide variety of things.

5 years

By the time a child reaches the age of five years they have become adept at understanding how other people may be feeling and are capable of hiding their own feelings. At five years of age children are usually very good at controlling their emotions.

6–8 years

Between the ages of six and eight years children often put a lot of emphasis on wanting to succeed and can often become very competitive. This competitiveness becomes apparent when quarrels begin to surface more and more frequently as the child becomes increasingly demanding and stubborn.

8 years and over

Children begin to experience a variety of mood changes as they grow in years and develop. They may still show competitiveness but will often rely more on diplomacy than quarrels as they become more and more mature. Peer approval is important to children of this age and the need to succeed and become accepted is rated highly.

Communication and Language Development

0–3 months
From birth to three months the only language a baby is capable of is either crying, gurgling or cooing. Although unable to communicate verbally they will recognize and respond to sound.

3–6 months
Babies of this age have now learned to laugh and may imitate the sounds they recognize.

6–9 months
Babbling noises will continue and increase and the baby may be able to make simple sounds such as 'ee' or 'ah'.

9–12 months
Although unable to form sentences themselves, a child between nine and twelve months may be able to respond to simple instructions such as 'kiss mummy'. Children of this age can successfully be taught to imitate the sounds of animals for example 'woof', 'meow', 'baa', etc.

1 year
By the time a child reaches their first birthday they will have begun to use basic sounds and simple words. Children of this age are beginning to talk and may be able to say 'mama' and 'dada'.

2 years
It is thought that a child of two years of age will have developed a vocabulary of around 50 words. Although they may only actually use this number of words themselves whilst communicating, they will in fact understand many more. Children of this age learn to talk at a rapid speed and enjoy taking part in conversations.

3 years
Children of three years are able to speak in sentences using past and present tenses and plurals. They may become increasingly frustrated at this age by their inability at times to express themselves verbally. Children of three years enjoy listening to stories, singing songs and reciting rhymes, and repetition is usual.

4 years

By the time a child has reached their fourth birthday they will have become very inquisitive, wanting to know about many things. They will constantly ask questions and seek explanations.

5 years

The child's vocabulary has increased dramatically by the time they reach their fifth birthday and they will have become very confident speakers. The child will be adept at understanding the meaning of a large number of words even if they do not use the words themselves.

6–8 years

By the time a child reaches this age they will be able to describe things accurately. They should be able to give opposites and recognize similarities.

8 years and over

By now the child will be using a much wider vocabulary of words and more complex meanings. They will be able to speak using tenses and explain things confidently.

Intellectual Development

0–3 months

From birth to three months babies have the ability to focus on objects up to a few inches away from themselves. They will 'root' and turn towards the smell of the breast. They will listen to voices and try to make eye contact.

3–6 months

Babies of this age are beginning to develop their coordination, they enjoy bright colours and shiny objects and will reach out for interesting objects.

6–9 months

By the time a baby reaches this age they will be able to take part in simple games such as peek-a-boo. They will need to be stimulated more and should be offered interesting and more complex objects in order to keep them amused.

9–12 months

A child's memory is beginning to develop at this age and they will have the ability to remember things. They may be able to clap their hands and wave goodbye. They will enjoy imitating those around them, including their actions, the sounds they make and the moods they express. Often at this age a child will laugh if they see others laughing and cry if they see others are upset, without actually knowing why they are expressing these particular moods.

1 year

By the time a child has reached their first birthday their intellectual development will have increased greatly. They will be competent at focusing on particular aspects and will begin to understand that people have different preferences.

2 years

Children around the age of two years enjoy 'pretend' play and will often talk to themselves and act out fantasies. They may enjoy music and be adept at making sounds themselves from a variety of instruments.

3 years

The pretend play a child discovers at around the age of two will continue, develop and become more complex. Concentration will increase. Fine motor skills will have developed, enabling the child to control a pencil and paintbrush more easily, and they may even be able to cut paper using a pair of scissors.

4 years

By the time a child reaches the age of four their memory will be developing very quickly and they will be able to understand the concept of past and future. They will be able to master intricate activities such as threading beads on string, building towers with small blocks and holding a pencil with accuracy. Their drawings will be recognizable.

5 years

The concepts of literacy and numeracy are beginning to take hold by the time children reach their fifth birthday and many children of this age will be able to count confidently and recognize simple words. They become increasingly interested in everything around them and will probably ask endless questions.

6–8 years

Between the ages of six and eight years the child's reading and mathematical skills will have developed considerably and they will be able to read and write independently.

8 years and over

As the child progresses through school they will become more and more confident and their intellectual development will increase with the knowledge they are fed. They will take a broader view of the world around them and they will develop ways to expand on their own ideas.

Physical Development

0–3 months

From birth to three months a baby will lie on its back. The head will fall forward and the back curves. Towards the end of this stage the baby will start lifting his or her head and will be able to kick vigorously. They will be able to watch the movement of their own hands and play with their fingers. Babies in this age group recognize bright lights, loud noises and shiny objects. They will also recognize the face of their main carer.

3–6 months

By now the baby will be able to grasp objects and transfer them from one hand to the other. They will be able to control their head reasonably well and will attempt to put objects in their mouth.

6–9 months

Between the ages of six and nine months babies will usually be able to roll from their front to their back. They may also be attempting to crawl and will be able to grasp their feet.

9–12 months

Mobility usually comes to babies at around this age. They will probably be able to get around by either rolling, shuffling or crawling and may even be able to walk unaided. They may be able to sit unaided for considerable lengths of time and they should be able to grasp, hold and throw toys.

1 year

By the time a baby reaches its first birthday there is a good chance that they will be mobile either by crawling or walking. Although maintaining balance will still be difficult, most babies of this age can manage to climb stairs (under supervision) and will be able to kneel without support and pull themselves into a standing position using furniture.

2 years

Children at two years of age should be very mobile. They will be able to walk and run and should be able to negotiate steps and stairs, although this will probably be with two feet at a time. They will be able to throw and kick a ball but may not be confident at catching.

3 years

Children of this age will have learnt how to master most methods of movement. They will be able to run, walk forwards, backwards and sideways, jump from low heights, balance on one foot and walk on tiptoe. By now they should also be able to negotiate stairs and steps with one foot at a time and have mastered how to ride a tricycle.

4 years

Physical development has usually come on in leaps and bounds by the time a child reaches their fourth birthday and they should now be able to catch, kick, throw and bounce a ball. They should be confident with balance and be able to walk along a straight line.

5 years

By the time a child is five years old they should have mastered how to use a variety of equipment and their physical ability will be greatly enhanced. They will be confident playing simple ball games and able to hop, skip and move to music. Their fine motor skills will have improved greatly and their drawings will begin to resemble their intended objects.

6–8 years

By the time a child has reached their eighth birthday, they should have the confidence to jump from heights, run distances and ride a bicycle without stabilizers. Their balance and agility will have increased enormously by this age.

8 years and over

As children get older their physical development will improve along with their confidence. They will become more and more willing to try out new things and will begin to stretch themselves further. They will be confident playing complex games and taking part as a team member.

Factors which Affect Growth and Development

There are a great number of factors which affect a child's growth and development and studies have shown that these can be divided into three separate categories:

1 Antenatal – from conception to birth
2 Perinatal – during actual birth
3 Postnatal – after birth.

The majority of the factors which affect a child's growth and development are found in the postnatal category; these include:

- Allergies to food
- Health problems including infection
- Nutrition
- Environment, including overcrowding and pollution
- Poverty
- Lack of appropriate areas to play both indoors and out, along with appropriate toys for stimulation

- Serious accidents resulting in the loss of limbs or the use of senses
- Culture
- Loss or bereavement
- Separation or divorce of parents
- Learning difficulties
- Social factors such as love and affection.

Food Allergies

Food allergies in children are very common. Some allergies, such as intolerance to nuts and/or shellfish which may cause the body to go into an anaphylactic shock, are very severe and can be fatal. An anaphylactic shock is when the airways swell up and the child has difficulty breathing.

Another potentially life-threatening condition is diabetes. Diabetic children usually have to avoid sugar in their diet. It is absolutely essential that children with this condition have regular, well-balanced meals. A child can go into a diabetic coma or seizure if the sugar levels in the blood get too low.

Asthma and eczema are also very common in children and may be aggravated by some foods. Dairy products in particular have been known to trigger these conditions.

Hyperactivity and the inability to concentrate are other conditions that affect some children and studies have shown that these behavioural problems are due to intolerance to the yellow food dye tartrazine, which can be found in many soft drinks and sweets.

Children may also be intolerant of gluten. Gluten is found in cereal products and people with this kind of intolerance are usually referred to as coeliacs.

Health

The list of health problems that can affect a child's growth and development is huge and can range from simple colds and ear infections, which are short-lived, to much more serious problems such as cystic fibrosis, which can be life threatening. If you are caring for a child with a particular health problem it is absolutely vital that you work with the parents to provide the best care possible for the child. You will need to glean as much information as you can about the child's condition in order to plan for their care and well-being. Parents will be very knowledgeable about any condition that affects their child and they are the best people to ask for advice and information. However, you may also like to source further information from doctors, health visitors and the internet.

Serious infections such as whooping cough and measles can have repercussions on a child's health.

Exercise

Where could you go for help and information if you agreed to take on the care of a child with cystic fibrosis?

Nutrition

Childminders should always discuss with the parents of the children in their care which meals they will be expected to provide and what food should be given. It is absolutely paramount when preparing meals that childminders take into consideration factors such as culture and religion and ensure that the food they provide is in keeping with the parents' wishes. For example, a parent wishing to bring their child up on a vegetarian diet must feel confident that you will prepare suitable meals for their child. Likewise a child whose family practises a certain religion or is from another culture should have their dietary wishes respected.

Children need to be given a healthy, balanced diet in order to grow and develop. There are five important nutrients which must be provided to encourage a healthy body and acceptable rate of growth. These are:

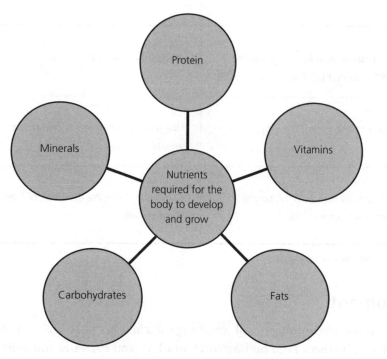

Figure 2.2 Essential nutrients required by the body

- Protein is found in meat, fish, poultry, vegetables, soya, tofu, quorn and dairy products.
- Vitamins are found in fresh fruit and vegetables.
- Fats are found in meat, fish, dairy products and vegetable fats.
- Carbohydrates are found in bread, potatoes and vegetables.
- Minerals are found in meat and green vegetables. The mineral calcium is found in milk and other dairy products. It is essential that the diet contains these minerals as they cannot be manufactured by the body.

Each of the above nutrients plays a very important part in the body's growth and development and the chart below underlines the specific job each encourages within the body.

Protein Consists of building blocks known as amino acids	Encourages the body to grow Assists the body's healing process
Vitamins Two groups of vitamins known as fat soluble, such as A, D, E and K, and water soluble, such as C and B	Essential for the body's growth and development
Fats Unsaturated fats derived from vegetable sources and saturated fats from animal sources	Provide the body with energy
Carbohydrates Include starches and sugars	Like fats, carbohydrates provide the body with energy
Minerals Include calcium, sodium, sulphur, potassium, magnesium and trace elements	Calcium and iron are essential for growth and development

Figure 2.3 The function of nutrients

Environment

A loving, caring environment will encourage a child to socialize and develop good relationships with others. Poor housing, overcrowding, and air, water and noise pollution all have a detrimental effect on a child's growth and development.

A rural environment may also pose problems if there is high unemployment or people on low incomes. A lack of public transport and housing may also have an effect.

Poverty

It is estimated that approximately 2.5 million children in the UK live in poverty. Poverty puts children at a social disadvantage because parents who are unemployed or on low incomes may find it more difficult to provide a nutritionally balanced diet. They also tend to live in poorer housing which may often be overcrowded, and they generally lack the physical and personal resources to provide for their children.

Lack of Appropriate Play Areas and Toys

Children need to be active, involved and motivated in order to grow and develop. Their brains and bodies need to be suitably stimulated with areas to play, both indoors and out, and toys and equipment appropriate to their age and stage of development. Progress will be slow and impaired if there is a lack of stimulation.

Serious Accidents Resulting in the Loss of Limbs or the Use of Senses

A serious accident which results in the loss of one or more limbs or impairment to the senses may have a permanent effect on a child's growth and development. Less serious accidents may result in developmental delays such as becoming clingy and withdrawn.

Culture

Childminders must always respect a child's cultural background regardless of whether the culture is their own or not. They should use their knowledge and understanding to encourage children to learn about other cultures in a positive way.

Loss or Bereavement

Children often find it difficult to put things into perspective and may view the loss of a favourite teddy bear on the same level as the death of a close relative. Children suffering from the anxieties of loss or bereavement may try to hide their feelings for fear of upsetting those around them, while others will show their feelings freely. Signs of aggression and/ or withdrawal are often associated with the way children deal with their emotions when experiencing loss or bereavement.

Separation or Divorce of Parents

The areas of development most likely to be affected by the breakdown of relationship between a child's parents are social and emotional. Separation or divorce can make children become anxious and frightened. Their whole world, as they know it, will have been turned upside down and they may experience feelings of guilt, anger and sorrow. They may become withdrawn and tearful or aggressive and argumentative.

Childminders must work with the parents to find suitable ways to help the child through this difficult period. It is absolutely paramount that you do not take sides or apportion blame. Make sure you are there for the child if they need someone to talk to, but never probe or ask questions.

Learning Difficulties

Childminders who have agreed to take on a child with learning difficulties must work closely with the child's parents in order to provide the best possible care. Learning difficulties are numerous and can affect all areas of a child's growth and development. The difficulty in question may be obvious and the parents will tell you about it from the outset. There may, however, be times when you are caring for a very young baby and a learning difficulty becomes apparent to you for the first time; for example, you may notice that the child has difficulty hearing certain sounds or seeing things from a distance. In cases such as these, never be tempted to ignore the problem but speak sensitively to the parents and suggest that they seek expert help and advice.

Social Factors

Children starved of love and affection will find it difficult to develop and form good relationships with others. They may be untrusting, miserable and unhappy, and although they may appear physically healthy, they will be emotionally unwell. A child who has suffered from abuse will have their health and well-being severely affected and abuse can have long-lasting health implications.

Exploring the Senses

Very young babies rely heavily on their senses to learn; however, as they grow older learning in this way becomes less dominant. As a child carer you should allow the children the opportunity to use all their senses in order to explore and experiment in play. Generally speaking, babies and toddlers will use their senses instinctively to explore the things around them; however, it may sometimes be necessary for you to support a child who has a sensory impairment.

Exercise

Observe a baby or toddler while they are playing. Watch what they do with the toys you have provided for them. How frequently does the child put an object in their mouth?

It is very important that children are encouraged to use their senses to the full. In order to do this we must offer them a variety of broad experiences which will enable them to use sight, sound, touch, taste and smell. A well-structured learning environment, both indoors and out, is vital in order for the senses to develop naturally. As a child carer you will need to provide the children with a broad range of sensory experiences in order to enable them to explore and develop their own sensory awareness and, equally as important, to have empathy with those who may have sensory impairments.

What exactly are 'sensory experiences'?

- Sensory experiences are those experiences which involve the child using one or more of the five senses, i.e. sight, sound, touch, taste and smell.
- Sensory experiences can be planned or unplanned.
- Sensory experiences can take place both indoors and out.

Exercise

Think of an unplanned, spontaneous experience that a child may enjoy which would promote each of the five senses. For example, the feel of sand between the toes or the smell of fresh bread baking.

In the first few months of their lives, babies rely very heavily on three of the senses, namely taste, touch and smell. Rattles, fingers, toes and toys are all taken into the mouth from the age of a few weeks because this is how the baby explores.

A *treasure basket* enables a young child to explore all of the senses and is an excellent source of entertainment. It will provide a child with lots of opportunities to stimulate the five senses. Treasure baskets can be successfully used once the baby can sit up and consist of about 15 to 20 objects made of natural material, which have been carefully chosen for their texture and shape. The equipment should be clean and perishable objects replaced regularly. Always make sure that the objects you choose are appropriate for the child's age and avoid small items which can be inserted in the nose or ears or which may pose a choking hazard. Items you may like to consider for a treasure basket are:

- A small mirror
- A clean, dry fir cone
- A pumice stone
- A small natural sponge
- A large shell
- An orange
- A clothes peg
- A ball of crumpled tissue paper
- A piece of foil
- A large pebble

Sight

It is very important when planning activities that promote the sense of sight to remember that not all children have perfect vision and you must consider ways to involve both children with good vision and those who may have an impairment. The children in your care may be long-sighted, short-sighted, partially sighted or even completely blind.

When considering activities to promote the sense of sight, think about providing materials and resources that are brightly coloured and shiny. Think about taking older children on a visit to the optician or, if possible, introduce them to a visually impaired person who may rely heavily on a guide dog. Encourage the children to learn about the work of guide dogs by allowing them to visit the Guide Dogs for the Blind Association website. The Association provides information packs which contain excellent learning material. Introduce different words associated with sight such as wink, blink, peer, view, glimpse, and teach children the correct names for the parts of the eye such as the pupil and iris.

Exercise
Plan two activities, one indoors and the other outdoors, which would be suitable for promoting the sense of sight in a child of two years.

Sound

The use of the hearing sense is vital for the development of speech, language and, of course, listening. You may be caring for a child who is profoundly deaf, partially deaf or suffering from a temporary hearing loss, perhaps due to a heavy cold or infection. In today's society children are brought up in a busy, noisy atmosphere where many sounds are often competing against each other. We have become adept at filtering out certain sounds and have developed the skill of focused listening known as *auditory discrimination*. However, if a child is suffering from any kind of hearing impairment they may have difficulty in filtering out unwanted sound and it is for this reason that you should try to provide a calm learning environment where distractions are kept to a minimum.

When exploring the sense of sound, consider using music. Complicated and hi-tech instruments do not necessarily have to be used because young children will enjoy making music themselves using wooden spoons and pans or simple instruments such as tambourines, triangles and maracas.

Introduce new words to the children's vocabulary such as loud, soft, noisy, whisper, rattle, piercing etc.

Exercise

Plan two activities, one indoor and one outdoor, suitable for promoting the sense of sound in a child aged two years.

Touch

Children are naturally tactile and often enjoy receiving and giving cuddles and hugs. Touch features very heavily in the exploration of young children, who are by nature inquisitive. As a child carer you should allow the child to explore their sense of touch through a variety of materials while taking part in both 'wet' and 'dry' activities. Consider providing the children with malleable materials such as play dough and clay which they can mould and change in appearance. Other tactile materials which you could like to consider may be:

Dry activities	Wet activities
Dry sand	Play dough
Sawdust	Clay
Straw	Shaving foam
Grass/leaves	Mud
Rice/pasta	Flour and water
Shredded paper	Wet sand
Dry compost	Finger paints

Figure 2.4 Tactile materials

Exercise

Plan two activities, one indoor and one outdoor, suitable for promoting the sense of touch in a child of two years.

Taste

The sense of taste and smell are closely related and often a child who does not like the smell of something will also say they do not like the taste of it. However, it is important to encourage children to differentiate between the two senses in order to use them fully and explore the world around them.

The four primary tastes which are important to us are:

- sweet
- sour
- salt
- bitter

Each of these tastes is important for different reasons.

Sweet has developed through our search for energy.
Sour warns us against food that has been spoiled.
Salt enables us to maintain the body's essential fluids.
Bitter warns the body about the dangers of poisons and toxins.

Consider having a 'tasting session' in which children are blindfolded and encouraged to smell and taste a variety of foods. Ask the children to try to guess what the food is, prior to tasting, simply by using their sense of smell. Some foods, such as oranges, which have a strong smell will be easier to recognize than, say, an apple which has less of an aroma. Before undertaking any tasting activities always make sure that you have taken into account any allergies or dietary preferences which a child may have.

Introduce new words associated with taste to the child's vocabulary, such as sweet, sour, bitter, tangy, delicious etc.

> ### Exercise
> Plan a tasting session suitable for a child of two years of age who has a nut allergy. Consider using a particular group of foods such as fruit and introduce less common fruits such as figs and kiwi alongside apples and bananas.

Smell

As mentioned previously, the sense of smell is closely linked with that of taste. However, children should be encouraged to explore the world around them using both these senses separately, because not all 'smells' can be 'tasted'. Encourage children to discuss the different smells they have experienced; for example, how a doctor's surgery or dentist may smell 'clinical' and how a restaurant or café may smell 'appetizing'. Encourage the children to smell different things such as herbs and spices, soap, coffee, vinegar, flowers, grass cuttings etc.

Introduce new words to the child's vocabulary to describe the different types of smells such as spicy, fresh, scented etc., and discuss smells that may warn of danger, such as smoke.

> ### Exercise
> Plan two activities, one indoor and one outdoor, which would be useful for promoting the sense of smell in a child aged two years.

Wherever possible you should be striving to offer the children a wide range of activities and experiences which will help them to explore their senses both individually and as a group. A child who lacks one or more of the senses or has an impairment will often compensate by developing more sophisticated working senses. For example, a child who has been born blind will develop a more defined sense of touch than a sighted baby, despite the fact that they both begin with the same potential for the sense of touch. This is because the blind baby will compensate for his or her lack of sight by decreasing the area of the brain assigned to sight and concentrating more on the area assigned to touch.

In addition to a treasure basket, another useful resource which encourages the child to use and develop all of the senses is a sensory garden. Although all children would enjoy visiting a sensory garden and gain some skills from it, children with a sensory impairment would benefit tremendously. If you are caring for a child with one or more sensory impairments you would be well advised to consider creating this type of garden for yourself. The area need not be huge or very complex and can be achieved in a small garden.

Creating a Sensory Garden

Ideally the whole of the garden should be used in order to allow the child the freedom to wander and explore. However, a sensory garden can also be effective if confined to a specific area of the garden.

Sight
The sense of sight can be explored in a garden by using a variety of:

- coloured pots and tubs to display plants and seeds
- coloured bark, paving or pebbles to define certain areas
- colourful plants and shrubs with interesting shapes such as sunflowers
- shrubs which encourage wildlife, such as a buddleia bush which attracts butterflies
- nectar-rich plants such as scabious, aubrietia and sedum which attract birds and insects.

Sound
The sense of sound can be explored in a garden by:

- planting a variety of plants and shrubs such as ferns and grasses which, when blown by the wind, make rustling or whispering noises
- hanging wind chimes made of bamboo or metal around the garden
- planting trees and shrubs which attract birds to the garden
- using slate chippings and pebbles to create paths which 'crunch' underfoot.

Touch
The sense of touch can be introduced into a garden by:

- Planting a variety of tactile plants, shrubs and trees. Look for trees which have very smooth or very rough barks. Plant evergreen shrubs with glossy leaves among heathers.

- Plant fine feathery ferns and ornamental grasses.
- Introduce a sand-pit into the garden and a water tray.
- If space is plentiful consider a small playground consisting of a scramble net and ropes alongside the more popular swing and slide.
- Use gravel, pebbles, bark and slate chippings to introduce texture in the garden.
- Use shells as decoration around the garden to add interest and structure.

Taste

The sense of taste can be introduced to the garden by:

- Planting a variety of fruit trees. These need not be very large as many apple, pear and cherry trees come in dwarf varieties.
- Encourage the children to plant strawberries and tomatoes in tubs and containers.
- Introduce herbs into the garden.

Smell

The sense of smell can be introduced to the garden by:

- Planting a variety of plants and shrubs which produce flowers or leaves which are highly scented, such as roses, lilies, honeysuckle, sweet peas and lavender.
- Plant a herb garden with herbs such as mint, which has a strong smell.
- Use bark chippings along paths and around plants which smells differently when both wet and dry.
- Arrange pine cones around the garden.

Any garden, no matter how small, can incorporate sensory features to keep children of all ages entertained.

Remember

Children should be supervised at all times while playing outdoors, and although water can be a very useful learning commodity, it can also be extremely dangerous to young children who can drown in only a few inches of water. If you introduce water into your garden, make sure that children are supervised *at all times* when using it and that the water is emptied immediately after play has ceased.

Nature/Sensory Walk

If introducing a sensory garden is impractical you might like to consider taking the children on a nature walk which can be used to heighten the senses and encourage the children to enjoy their natural surroundings. Plan your walk in an interesting area which has a variety of things for the children to see, hear, touch, feel and smell. A woodland walk would be ideal as the children would be able to use their senses in a variety of ways such as smelling flowers, walking on different surfaces, listening to the sounds of the wildlife etc. These types of walks will enhance a child's awareness of their natural environment and you should encourage the children to talk about their experiences once you have returned to the setting. Allow the children to communicate their views by asking them:

- What did you see?
- What did you hear?
- What did you smell?
- What did you feel?
- What did you enjoy the most during the walk?
- What did you enjoy the least during the walk?

The activity can be extended with the use of cameras and recording equipment and the children can make displays on a table or record their findings in a book.

Exercise

Plan a sensory walk for the children in your care. Choose a suitable area for the walk such as a country lane, park or woodland and make a note of the things you hope to see, hear, smell, taste and touch which will benefit the children. Remember to take into account the time of year in which you are planning your walk as this can greatly alter the sensory factors; for example:

- in spring, the colours and scents of bluebells in the woods would be lovely to experience
- in the summer wildlife will be in abundance
- in the autumn the leaves will be changing colour and falling off the trees, they will be crisp underfoot
- in the winter frost and snow will change the scenery dramatically.

Useful Websites

www.asbah.org.uk
Association for Spina Bifida and Hydrocephalus

www.asthma.org.uk
Asthma UK

www.allergyfoundation.com
British Allergy Foundation

www.bcodp.org.uk
British Council of Disabled People

www.bda.org.uk
British Deaf Association

www.bdadyslexia.org.uk
British Dyslexia Association

www.diabetes.org.uk
Diabetes UK

www.disabilityalliance.org.uk
Disability Alliance

www.downs-syndrome.org.uk
Down's Syndrome Association

www.epilepsy.org.uk
Epilepsy Action

www.gdba.org.uk
Guide Dogs for the Blind Association

www.hacsg.org.uk
Hyperactive Children's Support Group

www.muscular-dystrophy.org.uk
Muscular Dystrophy Campaign

www.eczema.org.uk
National Eczema Society

www.meningitis-trust.org.uk
National Meningitis Trust

www.rnib.org.uk
Royal National Institute for the Blind

www.sicklecellsociety.org.uk
Sickle Cell Society

Planning and Supporting Children's Learning and Development

Planning is absolutely essential to the smooth running of any childcare business. In order to be able to work efficiently and effectively you will need to be organized and plan your working day and week. The way you choose to plan is entirely up to you as this is a personal choice. Some childminders have written plans while others prefer to rely on their memories. Providing the planning works effectively it does not matter how it is done. By putting pen to paper, however, you will be able to build up a resource of activities and experiences to refer back and add to. Written plans are also a good way of providing evidence of your professionalism and can be shared with parents and professional organizations such as Ofsted. Indeed, Standard 3 of the National Standards for Childminding in England refers directly to the childminder being responsible for 'planning and providing activities and play opportunities which will develop a child holistically'. Ofsted inspectors may well ask to see evidence of the way you plan your work and by getting into the habit of putting your plans down in writing you will have the relevant evidence to support this particular standard.

To plan means to prepare, set up and organize activities or experiences for the children. It is crucial to remember that how you plan is purely a matter of personal choice; the way in which you plan your day may well be very different from that of other childminders. There is no right or wrong way to plan, and providing your plans are effective, they should be acceptable.

When planning your day, there are certain things you will need to bear in mind for the children in your care. You will need to:

- Decide, with the parents of the children in your care, what you and they would like to see the child achieve.
- Decide on the child's and the parents' goals.
- Decide the time-scale within which these goals should be achieved.

By looking at the points above you will be able to decide whether you will need to make a long-, medium- or short-term plan.

Long-term plans
This type of planning can be spread over the course of a year. Long-term planning is a good way of covering all areas of growth and development for, say a two year old, and it will enable you to take into account events and festivals over an extended period of time.

Medium-term plans
This type of planning usually extends over a period of 3 to 4 weeks.

Short-term plans
This type of planning can be used for a specific activity or perhaps for a full day or week's activities.

Long-term plan	You may decide on a long-term plan of say 6 weeks to encourage a three-year-old child to recognize the colours red, blue and yellow.
Medium-term plan	Your medium-term plan could be to spend two weeks on each colour helping the child to recognize them individually.
Short-term plan	Your short-term plan could consist of an activity which encourages recognition of the colours and leads on to the medium- and long-term curriculum plan (see examples of activities overleaf).

Figure 3.1 Long-, medium- and short-term plans

Colour activities for the colour yellow:

Bake buns and decorate with yellow icing

Paint pictures using yellow paint

Colour activities for the colour red:

Building towers using red blocks

Making models using red play dough

Wear something red for the day

Colour activities for the colour blue:

Spot blue cars when out walking

Collect as many blue objects from around the house as possible

Figure 3.2 Examples of short-term plans

All of the activities in the short-term plan would have the desired outcome of helping the child to recognize the three colours red, blue and yellow at the end of the planned period of time.

Some childminders and nannies like to plan the child's learning and development around topics and themes and, depending on the age of the child, this can be a very effective way of capturing their interest providing you take into account each child's individual preferences. If you do decide to use topics and themes, avoid restricting the children and always allow time for spontaneous activities and free play. The most important thing to remember when planning activities and experiences is that your plans must work for both you and the children in your care in order to make them effective. If they do not work then it is essential that you change them!

> ## Exercise
>
> Make a list of topics and themes around which you could appropriately plan your activities. Make sure you take into account the age and stage of development of the children in your care. You may like to consider themes such as the seasons of the year, or topics covering colours, time etc.

As mentioned previously, some childminders choose not to write down any plans and rely purely on their memory. However, it is still worth understanding the importance of curriculum plans. Plans will help you to decide on appropriate activities and encourage you to cover all aspects of the child's development and learning satisfactorily. Sometimes it is easy to forget some aspects or spend too much time on some areas at the expense of others. A well-thought-out curriculum plan will eliminate this problem.

Planned activities are those that you have thought about in advance. You will need to take certain things into account when planning these:

- the age of the child
- their stage of development
- the resources needed
- the time needed
- the role you wish to play.

Unplanned activities are unexpected and spontaneous and happen at random, such as building a snowman after a sudden downfall of snow or looking at a rainbow after a downpour. Spontaneous activities are also very valuable learning opportunities for children and you should always encourage this type of learning.

Resources

To enable you to plan and support children's learning and development successfully, you will need to know where to go in order to obtain appropriate resources and equipment. There are hundreds of suppliers of toys and equipment and it can, at times, be difficult to decide what to purchase and from whom.

You are the best toy a child can have; however, it is necessary to provide toys and equipment, suitable for the age and stage of development of the child, to allow them to explore and experiment. Toys need not be very expensive and quite often the basic toys are the ones which successfully encourage children to use their imagination. Simple resources such as dressing-up clothes and building bricks are more versatile than other toys which can only really have one use. Avoid purchasing expensive toys which are fashionable; when the 'fad' passes the toy will usually be discarded.

Although you can't be expected to have every toy in your setting or to provide for every child's whim, you should aim to have a selection of clean, interesting toys which appeal to children of a variety of ages and stages of development. There may be times when you wish to obtain a particular toy for a short period of time, for example, to introduce a child to hospitals pending a stay or to help them settle into a new school, and this is when toy libraries are useful. Toy libraries lend toys and equipment to child carers for an agreed length of time and a nominal charge. Toy libraries are also useful for sourcing specially adapted toys which may be more accessible for a disabled child but which could be very expensive for you to purchase. Your local Children's Information Service should be able to help you to source your nearest toy library.

In addition to toy libraries, you may like to consider sharing toys and equipment with other childminders. If you are a member of a childminding group, talk to other members to see if you can organize some kind of share scheme.

The basic toys you will probably need if you are caring for babies and young children are:

- A selection of clean rattles and soft toys
- Games and puzzles
- Building bricks and construction toys
- A selection of books with both paper and cardboard pages
- Paper, crayons, paints, collage materials
- Dressing-up clothes and role-play accessories.

The list above should be adapted and added to depending on the age and stage of development of the children. If you care for school-aged children in addition to babies and pre-school children, then the toys and resources you provide must reflect this. You should not expect older children to play with baby toys and vice versa.

Knowing what kind of toys and equipment to purchase is very important if you are to avoid expensive mistakes. When you are in a position to add to your toys and resources, talk to the children you are caring for, ask them what they would like you to buy and incorporate their wishes whenever possible. This way you can be sure that you are buying something which will be of interest to them.

> **Exercise**
>
> Make a list of the basic toys and resources you need for the children in your care. Which of these items do you already have? Which items do you need to buy or add to? Which items will you place on your 'wish list' to purchase when funds allow?

Although markets and jumble sales can be good places for sourcing inexpensive toys, you should be extra vigilant when buying in this way. Always check that the toys are in a clean state and in good repair. Check for the necessary safety symbols and never be tempted to purchase items with broken or missing parts.

Suppliers

Toys, games and other play equipment can be purchased from larger retailers such as Early Learning Centre, Toys 'R' Us and Mothercare.

A good selection of arts and craft materials can be purchased from Baker Ross, S & S Services and again from Early Learning Centre. 2 to 5.com is an online company providing a diverse selection of resources covering festivals and celebrations, ICT, sensory development, and equality, to name but a few and further details can be obtained by logging on to www.2to5.com or telephoning 0800 107 6094.

Kid Premiership Limited stock a good selection of children's books and educational material and these can be purchased online by visiting www.kidpremiership.com

Learning and Developing Through the Ages

Education has changed and developed greatly over the years and improvements to the National Curriculum throughout the United Kingdom are continually being made.

In England the National Curriculum consists of a Foundation Stage for children from 0 to 5 years and then four Key Stages as follows:

- Key Stage 1 (5–7 years of age)
- Key Stage 2 (7–11 years of age)
- Key Stage 3 (11–14 years of age)
- Key Stage 4 (14–16 years of age).

Children are assessed through Standard Assessments Tasks (SATs) at the end of each Key Stage.

The subjects across the four Key Stages are as follows:

- Core subjects
  - English
  - Mathematics
  - Science
- Foundation subjects
  - Design and Technology
  - History
  - Information Technology
  - Geography
  - Art
  - Music
  - Physical Education
  - Modern Languages.

In Wales, depending on whether Welsh is the child's first language, the children follow three or four core subjects. Children being educated in a Welsh-medium school will study English, mathematics, science and Welsh. Welsh is tested along with the other subjects at the end of each Key Stage, if it is taught as a key subject. Although Welsh is studied by all children up to Key Stage 3 the tests are optional if Welsh is not the child's first language. Although most of the subjects in the Welsh National Curriculum are the same as those in the English National Curriculum, there are a couple of differences: for example, modern languages and technology are optional at Key Stage 4.

The Scottish Curriculum has been designed largely by qualified teachers and allows the teachers to decide when a child is ready to move to the next level. In order to ascertain whether all teachers are using the same criteria appropriately, a sample of assessments are monitored. The results of the teacher's assessments are shared with the parents of the children.

The Scottish Curriculum covers six areas of learning:

- English
- Mathematics
- Science
- Design and Technology
- Creative and Expressive Studies
- Language Studies.

The Northern Ireland Curriculum has similarities with both the English and Scottish Curricula. It mirrors the English National Curriculum in that children are tested at the end of each Key Stage and it is similar to the Scottish Curriculum in its areas of study.

The Northern Ireland Curriculum covers the following areas of learning:

- English (at Key Stage 1 this includes drama and media studies)
- Mathematics
- Science
- Design and Technology
- Creative and Expressive Studies
- Language Studies (if Irish is offered, another modern language must also be made available).

0–5 Years

In 2002 the Birth to Three Matters framework was produced to support practitioners working with children from birth to three years. This framework encouraged practitioners to observe, reflect and plan their work in order to meet the needs of children. Scotland followed suit and in 2005 produced an approach to supporting the development of young children called 'Birth to Three – supporting our youngest children'. From September 2008 the Birth to Three Matters framework is to be replaced by the Early Years Foundation Stage (EYFS). The EYFS will be a single framework for care, learning and development for children in all early years settings from birth to the August after their fifth birthday. The EYFS builds on the existing Curriculum Guidance for the Foundation Stage, the Birth to Three Matters framework and the National Standards for Under 8s Day Care and Childminding.

The main aim of the EYFS is to help young children achieve the five *Every Child Matters* outcomes:

- Staying Safe
- Being Healthy
- Enjoying and Achieving
- Making a Positive Contribution
- Achieving Economic Well-being.

The principles of the EYFS guide the work of all practitioners and are grouped into four distinct themes:

- A Unique Child
- Positive Relationships
- Enabling Environments
- Learning and Development.

The principles, pedagogy and practice from Birth to Three Matters have been retained and each of the following Areas of Learning and Development reflect the existing 'stepping stones' approach to the Foundation Stage:

- Personal, Social and Emotional Development
- Communication, Language and Literacy
- Problem Solving, Reasoning and Numeracy
- Knowledge and Understanding of the World
- Physical Development
- Creative Development.

One of the most important aspects of a childminder's job is to ensure that children *enjoy* learning. It may be argued that, by introducing children to 'formal' learning at too young an age, it could be off-putting because the emphasis is on 'learning' rather than having 'fun'. A young child may well refuse to cooperate if they think they are being pushed too soon and no longer find the activities enjoyable and exciting but now see them as difficult or even boring. Bearing this in mind, the government has taken the advice of early years experts and published guidance on how children should be taught while they are at the Foundation Stage. It states that learning for young children should be a 'rewarding and enjoyable experience' which encourages them to 'explore, investigate, discover, create, practise, rehearse, repeat, revise and consolidate their developing knowledge, skills, understanding and attitudes'. It follows, therefore, that we should expect to see children learning while:

- Having fun
- Making friends
- Playing both inside and out
- Making decisions
- Making mistakes and being allowed to rectify them
- Being helpful
- Being independent.

England, Scotland, Wales and Northern Ireland each have their own set of guidelines for pre-school settings. Although the expectations are very similar in all four, there are differences in the detail and format of each.

The Scottish Curriculum Framework differs considerably from the English EYFS in terms of age specifications. The Scottish Framework is aimed at children between the ages of 3 and 5. It places emphasis on the following areas of a child's development:

- Play
- Emotional, personal and social development
- Communication and language
- Knowledge and understanding of the world
- Expressive and aesthetic development
- Physical development and movement
- Observation
- Equality of opportunity
- Supporting transitions, and valuing home and family.

The Welsh version of the Desirable Outcomes document was introduced by the Curriculum and Assessment Authority for Wales. The Welsh Desirable Outcomes emphasize the heritage of thinking about what makes good practice in the early childhood curriculum. The Curriculum and Assessment Authority for Wales has now decided to remove Standard Assessment Tasks (SATs) at the end of Key Stage 1 and these children will now follow an extension of the curriculum for the Foundation Stage, effectively following the same curriculum from 3 to 8 years.

The National Council for Curriculum and Assessment (NCCA) in Northern Ireland has begun to develop a national Framework for Early Learning. This follows a consultation on the discussion paper 'Towards a Framework for Early Learning', which was launched in March 2004. The Framework for Early Learning aims to ensure that all children are adequately supported in their learning and to bring more coherence to learning throughout early childhood.

Some of the remaining chapters of this book cover the key areas of children's learning and development and they will assist and support you with planning play and activities for the children in your care. The key areas of children's learning and development are as follows:

- Personal, Social and Emotional
- Communication, Language and Literacy
- Problem Solving, Reasoning and Numeracy
- Knowledge and understanding of the world
- Physical
- Creative.

5–7 Years

Quite often childminders provide care for school-aged children alongside babies and toddlers. Caring for children of school age could be either before or after school, during the school holidays, or all three. Although it is not the job of a childminder to deliver the National Curriculum to school-aged children, you will, however, be expected to provide suitable support for the children.

You may need to change your routines to accommodate school-aged children in your setting, particularly in school holidays. To enable you to support the learning of school-aged children in your setting you will need to:

- Provide a quiet area for the children to study and complete their homework. In order for the older children to have the time and space to do their homework without being disturbed, you will need to think about the area you provide for them and also ensure that the younger children in your care are suitably entertained in order to prevent them from disturbing the older ones.
- Understand the National Curriculum yourself! It is impossible for you to provide the support needed by school-aged children if you do not have a basic understanding of the National Curriculum. Quite often schools send information home with the children to give help and advice to their parents. Ask the school for an extra copy of the guidance to keep in your setting. Information sessions are very popular at schools throughout the UK when parents and carers are invited into school to be given information about the way their children are taught and how homework should be completed. Try to get along to one of these information sessions if possible.
- Encourage children to recognize, understand and deal with peer pressures such as bullying, smoking etc. Encourage the children to talk about their worries and help them get things into perspective without undermining their fears. Always discuss any concerns you may have with the child's parents.
- Explore the facilities in your area. Caring for a number of mixed-age children can be demanding and exhausting. Think carefully about how many children you can reasonably cope with and be realistic. If you want to get out and about during the summer holidays this will be much more achievable if you have three children than if you have eight!

Exercise

Ask at your local school for details of information sessions referring to Curriculum Guidance.

7–11 Years

The development of children between these ages is considerably slower than in their early years. They will, however, continue to grow in height and weight and will become more competent in reading, writing and numeracy skills. They will be able to play in an organized way and will know how to implement rules, play fairly and understand the importance of sharing. Strong friendships are usually forged at this age.

As a childminder you should be on hand to offer help and support to children as they carry out homework tasks. Supporting reading and spelling skills are just two of the areas where your help can be invaluable.

11–14 Years

Many physical changes occur in young people of this age. Their emotional and social development may be affected by the changes going on in their bodies, particularly if they are going through puberty.

Young people of this age respond well to responsibility and may need to exercise their independence more freely. They will need reassurance and approval and usually respond well to praise and encouragement.

It is common for children in this age group to develop insecurities. These may be about their school life, friends, appearance etc. and they will need reassurance. Although boundaries are necessary it is a good idea to involve children of this age in any rules you impose. Talk about the rules and why you think they are necessary. Allow the children to make their own contribution and listen to what they have to say. Negotiation can often prevent rebelliousness and later problems.

You should continue to offer help and support to the children in their homework tasks. Be aware that many children of this age begin to rebel and may even refuse to complete homework or, if it is completed, it is not done to a satisfactory level. Offer encouragement and, if necessary, speak to the child's parents if you have any concerns.

14–16 Years

When a person reaches this age group they are no longer a child but a young person facing decisions about their future. It is important for adults to take a step back and allow them to 'find themselves'. Listen to what they have to say and value their views and opinions.

As with younger children, continue to offer support and encouragement with regard to their school work.

Providing Play and Activities for Children of Different Ages

It is not always easy to plan and provide suitable activities if you are caring for children from different age groups. However, with thought and careful planning it is possible to keep all the children happy and entertained with resources and activities suited to their individual age and stage of development.

You must think carefully about the resources and materials you provide when caring for children of different ages and ensure that the things you supply for the older children do not pose a potential danger to the younger ones. Collage materials, for example, are often very useful for older children who have the ability to produce creative pieces of artwork using sequins, buttons, pompoms and shells; however, all these materials pose a choking hazard if they fall into the hands of young children. Adult supervision and the provision of a separate activity space for older children, away from babies and toddlers, are essential.

It may be very tempting to tell the older children that they cannot have certain toys or equipment out while the younger children are present but this is not always a good solution. The older children may only be in your care for a couple of hours after school, and if the baby or toddler is also present during these hours, then when can you allow the older children the chance to play with toys suitable for their own age? You should not expect the older children simply to conform and make do, as this will cause resentment and result in the older children becoming bored and gaining nothing from their time with you.

Exercise

Look carefully at the toys and equipment you have in your setting. Which items are suitable for *all* the children and which would need segregating? Plan how you can include all of the children in activities which are suitable for their individual age and stage of development without anyone having to compromise.

Planning and supporting children's learning does not have to mean lots of paperwork. As you gain more experience you will inevitably start to implement your plans instinctively without the need for much paperwork. Whether you choose to write down your plans or not is entirely up to you. However, what you must appreciate is the importance of this aspect of your job and understand that, as a childcare practitioner, you will be providing the children in your care with an important start to their formal years of learning. Part of your job as a home-based child carer is to educate the children in your care and you will be doing this all day, every day, either by providing the children with suitable toys, resources and experiences or by simply engaging them in everyday routines.

Regardless of the ages of the children you are caring for, there are three fundamental aspects of learning which you, as a childcare practitioner should recognize and put at the forefront of everything else. These aspects enable *all* children to learn:

- Language and communication (see Chapter 6 for more details)
- Play
- Firsthand experiences.

Learning through play should enable babies and young children to:

- Learn new skills and abilities
- Develop their existing skills and abilities
- Explore their environment
- Discover how things work
- Investigate and experiment
- Enjoy new experiences
- Develop a sense of belonging.

Supporting Children with Special Educational Needs (Including Gifted and Talented Children)

As caring for children from different age groups can be challenging, so too can caring for a child with special educational needs. When we talk about special educational needs we all too often think of children who need additional help perhaps due to learning disabilities or sensory impairment and while this is probably the most common example, it is by no means the only one. Gifted and talented children are equally likely to need additional support.

It is not always easy to define a child who has special needs. Sometimes the need is obvious, such as a child who has Downs Syndrome, but sometimes it is less apparent, as in the case of a child who has a particular talent. What defines each as having special needs is that they both need additional help in some areas of their development.

There are several categories for defining special needs:

- Chronic illness such as cystic fibrosis or asthma.
- Physical impairment such as mobility or coordination difficulties.
- Speech or language problems such as stuttering.
- Sensory impairment such as hearing or sight difficulties.
- Life-threatening illnesses such as AIDS or HIV.
- Behavioural difficulties such as hyperactivity or attention deficit hyperactivity disorder (ADHD).

- Giftedness relating to high academic achievements or artistically talented children.
- Specific learning difficulties such as dyslexia.
- Emotional difficulties such as depression or autism.

Gifted or talented children may also have additional educational needs. The two, although often grouped together, are different in definition. Gifted children are those who have a superior ability over a wide range of subjects. Talented children have a talent in a specific area of expertise, for example special musical aptitude or exceptional sporting prowess.

There are three approaches which may be adopted with regard to the education of gifted and talented children:

- *Acceleration.* The child is moved up a year in school. This is usually the obvious choice because the child can be placed in a class with children of a similar ability. Problems can sometimes occur in this approach, however, if the child suffers from any emotional effects as a result of being separated from their peer group.
- *Segregation.* The child is placed in a group of other children of the same age, who have an equally high ability. The children then follow a specialized curriculum suited to their ability.
- *Enrichment.* The child remains in their class but the curriculum is specially adapted to support and extend their particular abilities.

ICT offers endless opportunities for children who are gifted or talented to pursue individual interests and learn new skills. The internet can be used to expand activities and lessons for more able pupils. Powerpoint is designed to challenge children to take part in a problem-solving game based on a curriculum theme.

Observations and Assessments

Let us think carefully about what it actually means to observe and assess children. 'Observing' children means to watch them closely and study in detail what they are doing. 'Assessing' children means to sum up what you have observed and use the information you have gathered to provide for the children's needs.

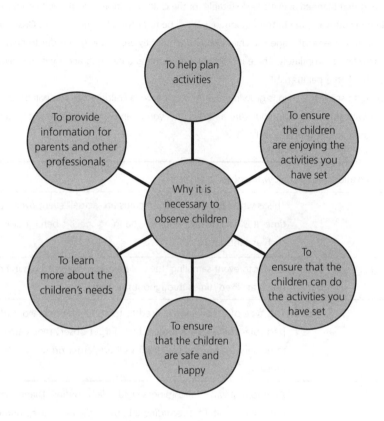

Figure 3.3 Why observation of children is necessary

There may be times when you will have to carry out more detailed observations on the children in your care rather than simply watching and examining what they are doing on a daily basis.

There are several reasons why home-based child carers need to observe children:

- Learning more about children's needs. By specifically observing one child at a time you will be able to identify any particular strengths or weaknesses they may have. You will be able to use your observations to produce evidence which may be needed to present to specialists, should the child require outside help.
- Sorting out any particular problems. It may be necessary, at times, for you to work with the parents of a child to help sort out a particular area of their development which is causing a problem, for example tantrums. Your observations will enable you and the parents to decide whether there is a genuine need for concern or not.

- Checking that planned activities are suitable for the child. The more information you have about the children in your care, the better equipped you will be to provide for their needs. Observing children allows you to see what stage the child is at and what they enjoy doing in order to help you to plan your activities appropriately. There is little point in planning a painting activity if the child has yet to master holding a paintbrush!
- Checking to see if the child is growing and developing. As a childminder you will be spending a lot of time with the children in your care and this puts you in an excellent position to check whether the children are progressing well.

Method of observation	How the observation works
Event sampling	This is when the childminder records an 'actual' event over a period of time. It is particularly useful for changing specific behaviour in a child such as tantrums.
Time sampling	Similar to event sampling, the childminder will record what a child is doing at 'fixed' times throughout the day.
Target child	This type of observation is used to focus on the behaviour of a particular child, i.e the *target* child. Target observations are usually used in nursery classes and playgroups where larger groups of children are present.
Diary	An informal way of recording a child's daily routine. Diaries are particularly useful for recording a baby's daily feed, sleep and nappy-changing patterns.
Flow chart	These are diagrams showing activities and equipment layout and, with the use of lines, can show which activities children take part in and enjoy. Flow charts eliminate the need for lots of writing and are quick and easy to implement.
Interval recording	Similar to time sampling, interval recording is useful for focusing on a specific issue with regard to a child's behaviour.
Participative observation	This type of observation requires the childminder to *take part* in the activity which can make recordings difficult to write. It is important, when relying on memory, to ensure your findings and recordings are accurate.
Non-participative observation	The opposite to participative observation. This is when the childminder does *not* take part in the activity but simply watches and records what they are witnessing.

Duration recording	This type of observation is good for recording how much interest a child shows in a particular activity.
Written observation	This type of observation is detailed and accurate and often time consuming to conduct.
Checklists and tick charts	An easy way to record a child's progress through simply ticking a chart listing appropriate milestones the child may have achieved.

Figure 3.4 Methods of observation

Balance Checklist	Name and age of child
Stands confidently on one foot	
Can balance on one foot for 5 seconds	
Can balance on one foot for longer	
Can walk along a straight narrow line	
Can weave in and out of cones	
Can walk up stairs both feet together	
Can walk up stairs one foot at a time	

Figure 3.5 Example of a tick chart for balance

In addition to *methods* of observations, childminders also need to be aware of *types* of observation. The main types of observation are:

- Naturalistic
- Structured
- Longitudinal
- Snapshot

Type of observation	How the observation works
Naturalistic	Observations carried out in the child's natural surroundings. Activities are not structured and the child is observed carrying out tasks they are familiar with.
Structured	Activities set up by an adult in order to observe how a child tackles a particular task.
Longitudinal	This is a set of records build up over a period of time showing the child's overall achievements and identifies the important milestones.
Snapshot	This is an observation done to record a child's immediate reaction to a particular scenario, for example to observe what happens prior to a child having a tantrum. A snapshot observation would recall the incident building up to the tantrum.

Figure 3.6 Types of observation

Whatever type of observation you opt for, all will require a certain amount of essential information:

- The name of the child
- The age of the child
- The date the observation was carried out
- The activity the child was involved in during the time the observation took place
- The number, ages and gender of any other children involved in the activity
- The name of the person carrying out the observation.

Written Observation

Name of child
Date of observation
Time of observation
Short description of what happened immediately prior to the tantrum

Short description of what happened during the child's tantrum
The outcome
Evaluation

Figure 3.7 Example of a written observation which could be used to record the events leading up to a child's particular behaviour; in this case a tantrum.

It is very important when carrying out observations that you record only the essential, accurate information in order for them to be beneficial. Always remain impartial and record *exactly* what you have witnessed without adding your own assumptions or opinions.

Useful Websites

More information about the National Curriculum for England can be found by visiting www.qca.org.uk

Details of the Early Years Foundation Stage can be obtained by visiting www.surestart.gov.uk

Details of the Ireland National Curriculum can be obtained by visiting www.ncca.ie

Details of Scottish Early Years education can be obtained by visiting www.ltscotland.org.uk

Details for the Welsh National Curriculum can be obtained by visiting www.wales.gov.uk

4 Social Development and Activities

Forming Relationships

Human beings are social animals and people, both children and adults, need other people. Everything we do is influenced by others; the way we think, move, feel and develop our ideas are all related to the way in which we are influenced by other people.

Although it is important that children learn how to communicate and respond to others in order for them to form lasting relationships, it is also vital that we allow them their own personal space. Together with companionship, human beings of every age also need to be alone sometimes and the need for personal space must be respected.

The main purpose of social development and encouraging the formation of relationships in young children is to prepare them for a life of living and working with others. Although certain social skills may be inborn, the majority of these skills have to be learned and this is done through experience.

It is surprising how often adults expect children to take new places and change in their stride; while some children do cope admirably with change, a great many are often nervous of unfamiliar people and places; this can be witnessed during a child's first day at school, for example. Children who have had the opportunity to mix and socialize from a young age often cope with this new transition better than those who have not, and it is unfair of us to expect a child who has had little experience of new situations to be confident when faced with them.

Exercise

Try to visit a primary school during the first few days of a new term. Note how the children respond to their new environment when

   a) their parents are present
   b) their parents have left.

What proportion of the children appear to settle quickly? How many of the children are visibly distressed?

By the time a child reaches their fourth birthday they are more than likely to have attended some form of pre-school setting such as a play group or nursery and will therefore have had some experience of socializing and mixing with others.

Although most young children are tolerant of other children, they do not usually begin to form friendships and interact together until the age of about four years. Prior to playing cooperatively, children usually watch and play alongside one another.

Children have an innate need to relate to others and, generally speaking, they have an intense desire to be liked and accepted by both adults and other children.

There are two main types of socialization:

- Primary socialization
- Secondary socialization

Primary socialization

This is the initial type of socializing in which a child becomes involved and it takes place within the home. This type of socialization involves learning from the family about what is and is not accepted within the home setting.

Secondary socialization

This is the next stage of socializing when a child learns about what is and is not accepted outside the family setting.

Quarrelling, taking part in disputes and learning to solve these disputes are all vital to a child's overall social development. It is important for the child carer to understand when to intervene in a dispute and when to step back and allow the children the chance to solve things for themselves. It can be very unhelpful if an adult, particularly one who has not witnessed the full extent of the disagreement, intervenes, and it will have a negative impact on the children if all their quarrels and disputes are solved for them. However, adult intervention should always take place if:

- A child is being bullied
- Physical violence is being used
- A child is being 'ganged up on' by several others
- Racist or discriminatory language is being used.

It is important to realize that while trying to encourage children to form positive relationships not everyone is destined to be best friends and it is impossible to make two children become firm friends if this is not their intention. Just as adults have preferences and may face personality clashes with others, so too do children and you should not expect them to form positive relationships with everyone they meet.

Exercise

Consider your own relationships for a moment. Who do you have a really strong relationship with and what makes this friendship special? Do you know someone that you clash with personally – could anything change the way you feel about this person?

Before a child can successfully begin to form good relationships with others it is essential that they develop a sense of self-esteem. They need to feel happy about themselves in order to feel confident within their community.

It is important to remember that a child's personal, social and emotional development cannot be met simply by offering a variety of occasional activities. It is achieved by ensuring that you, the childcare practitioner, are providing a daily routine that offers the child a safe and supportive environment in which their self-confidence can grow. Children need to be allowed the time to convey their own thoughts and feelings and should be encouraged to share their views and preferences; but above all they need the adults around them to listen to and value what they have to say.

Sense of Community

It is important that we encourage children to have positive attitudes about other people regardless of their race, gender, colour or ability. Children get their negative attitudes from the people and resources around them, and once these prejudices have been formed, they are difficult to change. Therefore it is essential that you provide the children with positive images and attitudes to enable them to grow up tolerant in our multicultural society. Some children will have frequent opportunities for mixing and socializing with other children whose culture, race and colour are different from their own, because they are living in a multicultural community themselves. However, this is not always the case, and for children who do not live in a multicultural community you will need to introduce them to different cultures and races through the resources and equipment you provide. Books and television can be invaluable for this purpose and will encourage children to develop positive attitudes as well as helping them to understand about adults and children with learning difficulties or sensory impairments.

Exercise

It is essential that children learn to develop positive attitudes towards adults and children with learning difficulties or sensory impairments. Although this cannot always be done through personal experience, how many of us personally know a blind or deaf person? Learning difficulties can be explored in other ways. Think about how you would introduce positive attitudes towards a child in a wheelchair.

Exploring Cultures and Religions

Where children live in a multicultural community, there will be frequent opportunities for them to learn from others about the religions, traditions and festivals that are important to different cultures. However, for those children who are not living in a multicultural community it is the responsibility of the adults around them to ensure that they learn what they need to know, and this can be done through careful planning. For children to understand, accept and respect other cultures and religions they need to know that:

- People communicate in different languages
- People dress in different ways
- People attend different schools
- People attend different churches
- People eat different food
- People share different beliefs.

Again, cultures, beliefs and nationalities can be explored by the use of certain resources such as books, posters and puzzles.

One of the best ways to explore cultures and religions is through the celebration of festivals. There are a great number of religious and cultural festivals celebrated throughout the world and some of these are also widely celebrated in the United Kingdom. The diversity of the society we live in today makes it important for us to be aware of the festivals which are celebrated by ethnic groups in addition to the Christian ones. The following list shows some of the religious and cultural festivals celebrated in the United Kingdom.

Religious and Cultural Festivals

- Harvest Festival
- Rosh Hashana (Jewish New Year)
- Sukkot (Jewish Harvest Festival)
- All Souls' Day
- Diwali (Festival of Light)
- Guy Fawkes Day
- Remembrance Sunday
- Thanksgiving
- Hanukkah (Jewish Festival of Light)
- Advent
- Easter
- Eid
- Holi (Festival of Colour)
- Chinese Lantern Festival
- April Fool's Day
- Lent
- May Day
- American Independence Day
- Christmas
- Rastafarian Christmas
- Chinese New Year
- Shrove Tuesday
- Ash Wednesday
- Mother's Day
- Father's Day
- Passover
- Ramadan
- St Patrick's Day
- St David's Day
- St George's Day
- Pentecost/Whitsuntide
- Chinese Festival of Hungry Ghosts
- Birthday of Mohammad

Knowing that their religion and culture are respected and acknowledged is vital for enabling children to feel accepted and welcome, and all children should be encouraged to explore not only their own culture and traditions, but also those of others. By introducing themes covering festivals and traditions you will successfully incorporate a method of encouraging children to understand and accept the diverse community in which we live. By celebrating festivals the children will have the opportunity to create objects using new and exciting materials. They will have the chance to take part in dressing-up and tasting a variety of foods enjoyed in other cultures, while developing their own ethical code. By encouraging children to celebrate a diverse mix of festivals and traditions you will help to give them all a sense of identity and boost their self-confidence.

Cultures and religions can be explored by introducing the following activities:

- Dressing-up: provide the children with a selection of clothes and materials from a variety of cultures, such as a sari or a kimono
- Books and stories explaining different traditions
- Puzzles showing a variety of cultures
- Making masks as part of celebrating a particular festival
- Making lanterns while celebrating the Chinese New Year

- Introducing craft work from other countries such as threading beads, knitting or tapestry
- Making flags which represent different countries.

Exercise

Choose a festival which you would like to celebrate with the children in your setting. Plan how you will celebrate your chosen festival, which resources you will use and what you hope the children will gain from the experience.

Equal Opportunities

Children learn values and attitudes by copying adults. One of the most important things you can do as a childcare practitioner is to provide the children with a positive role model. This means ensuring that you treat people fairly and equally at all times regardless of their age, gender, ability, ethnic or cultural background. Everyone is harmed by discrimination and prejudice.

People who are discriminated against are harmed because they are made to feel:

- Worthless
- Inferior
- Ashamed
- Different.

Someone who is discriminated against will lose their self-esteem and confidence and feel offended.

Likewise the people who express discrimination can also be harmed because they:

- Harbour false opinions of superiority
- Hold a distorted view of the world and the people living in it
- Miss out on opportunities to learn about our society as a whole.

The things we say and the way we act have a very definite effect on children and it is important that we do not force our own opinions and beliefs onto others. All too often people think that children don't notice the difference in skin colour, gender or ability but this is simply not true. Just as we teach children to recognize the colours of everyday objects such as the sun or the sky, they also learn to acknowledge the differences in the colour of people's skin.

One of the ways you, as a childcare practitioner, can avoid the negative effects of stereotyping and prejudice while working in your home-based setting, is to ensure that the children are surrounded by lots of positive images. You can do this by:

- Providing books and stories which show the 'hero' as disabled.
- Putting up posters around your setting which show positive images of women, black people and disabled people in challenging and responsible roles.
- Encouraging boys to play alongside girls in the home corner and dressing-up area.
- Encouraging boys to explore their emotional and creative side.
- Provide puzzles showing images of girls and women in strong, independent roles, and boys and men in caring roles for example a women firefighter alongside a male nurse.

Incorporating ICT

ICT can be successfully used to develop and explore social and emotional development in a number of ways:

- Karaoke: allow the children to stage a karaoke or singing concert with the help of a microphone and CD player. This will encourage the children to work together to plan the concert and sequence of songs.
- Make tape recordings of animal noises and play them back for the children to listen to and guess the animal. Allow the children to discuss their ideas.
- Allow the children to use walkie-talkies so that they can interact with one another from different rooms or while playing in the garden.
- Invest in one or two programmable toys that the children can learn to set up and utilize.
- Think about purchasing computer programs aimed at exploring emotions and feelings.

Exercise

Study the computer programs on sale which are aimed at children and note which of them you consider to be useful learning tools for promoting social development. Remember to take into account the age and stage of development of the children in your care.

Social Activity Ideas

There are many suitable activities which will successfully promote a child's social development. The list overleaf gives some ideas for activities which you may like to try with the children in your care. Try altering and extending the activities to suit the age and ability of the children.

Celebrating festivals	Choose a festival to celebrate and allow the children to dress up in relevant costumes, taste the food associated with the festival and make objects relating to the festival such as lanterns for Chinese New Year.
Colours of the world	Teach children about the diversity of colours; start by discussing skin tones and develop into how we use colours to describe feelings and emotions, for example: green with envy white with fear feeling blue (upset) seeing red (anger).
All about me	Encourage the children to make a scrap-book all about themselves. Allow them to bring photographs from home and to use the book to describe their home, family, pets, friends, likes and dislikes. The books can then be used to encourage the children to tell others about themselves.
Playing games	Any kind of participative game is good for encouraging social development because the children learn to share, take turns and win or lose graciously. Team games and games played in groups, such as 'pass the parcel', are particularly good at encouraging children to take turns. Board games such as snakes and ladders, ludo and Monopoly are also good for encouraging children to take turns.
Home corner	Allowing the children opportunities for role play and dressing-up encourages them to explore their own identity and to participate in imaginary play with others.
Group discussions	Taking the time to discuss the day's events together as a group is an ideal way of encouraging children to express their own thoughts and views and to listen while others do the same.

Figure 4.1 Activities to promote social development

Useful Websites

www.scholastic.co.uk

Books and resources

www.teacherstuff.org.uk

Ideas on teaching children

www.teachingideas.co.uk

Ideas on teaching children at Foundation Level

www.thebigbus.com

Interactive learning for 3–11 year olds

www.funwithspot.com

Ideas to promote literacy, numeracy and ICT skills

www.ghbooks.com/activity

Early education books

www.theideabox.com

Education and activity resources

www.kidpremiership.com

Books and learning resources

www.mape.org.uk

Education through ICT

www.kids-channel.co.uk

Fun educational ideas and online games

www.kidsdomain.com

Fun educational ideas and online games centred around themes

www.tts-shopping.com

Learning resources for children

Emotional Development and Activities

Recognizing and Dealing with Emotions

Young children often find their emotions difficult to deal with. The strong urges and desires they feel can sometimes be quite frightening and difficult to control. Play can be used successfully as an outlet for children's emotions. Allowing a child to run around outside or kick a football, for instance, will help them to release pent-up anger and frustration in a constructive way rather than by resorting to throwing toys, smacking, kicking or biting. Recognizing a child's emotions and providing the activities and resources for them to deal with these emotions will teach a child how to control their feelings in a constructive way.

Exercise

What activities and resources would you give to a child who was:

1. Angry and frustrated?
2. Needing to be comforted?
3. Over-excited and needing to be calmed down?
4. Wanting to show love and affection?

Although distractions and comfort objects such as dummies and soft toys can play a large part in dealing with a child's emotions and avoiding confrontations, it is important to remember that sometimes a child's feelings are so strong and overpowering that none of the usual distractions will be effective. In cases such as these the child may well be confused and frightened by the intensity of their feelings and you will need to be on hand to calm the child and offer reassurance.

The way in which a child learns to deal with their emotions will depend, to a large extent, on the challenges they have faced in their lives. Children find ways of coping with situations or people that may have upset or angered them. Play enables them to come to terms with events in their own lives and encourages them to experiment in the way that they themselves relate to others.

Children should be encouraged to recognize, explore, talk about and deal with their emotions. Emotional outbursts or 'tantrums' are usually the product of frustration. A child who is experiencing strong emotions but who lacks the language skills to express adequately the way they are feeling may well resort to a tantrum. It is important that the adults around them provide the necessary support to deal with these outbursts effectively. Remember that in a childminding setting there may often be other children present who will be affected by an emotional outburst; how you deal with this type of behaviour will also have an impact on them.

- Other children may be confused and not understand why the child is having a tantrum; you will need to offer reassurance and a simple explanation.
- The child who is exhibiting a tantrum may be kicking out; you will need to ensure the safety of the other children in the setting by removing the child who is having the outburst from the situation.

There are, of course, many more emotions which children experience in addition to anger and frustration. Excitement can be just as difficult to control as anger and many children show unacceptable behaviour when they are nearing a birthday for example, or when Christmas is looming.

> ### Exercise
> Think about the behaviour of a child who is nearing their third birthday. They have handed out their invitations and the day for their party is imminent. How would you expect the child to behave? Why would you expect to see this kind of behaviour?

Distress is another common emotion which children find very difficult to articulate. What appears to be inconsequential to us can be a major event to a young child and it is important that you never ridicule or undermine a child's feelings of distress. Losing a favourite toy, for example, can be just as distressing to a young child as the death of a grandparent. The concept of death may not be fully understood, while the absence of a much loved toy can be devastating.

As a childminder or nanny it is vital that you are able to effectively recognize the symptoms of distress within a child.

Possible signs of distress:

- Showing clingy behaviour, not wanting to leave a parent or carer.
- Refusing to join in games.
- Showing withdrawn behaviour and wishing to be alone.
- Reduced appetite or binge eating for comfort.
- Wetting or soiling themselves.
- Showing signs of bullying others.
- Regression in behaviour or habits, for example requesting a dummy even if they haven't had one for several months.

The reasons for distress in a child may be many and varied. A child may show one or more of the above signs if they have:

- Lost a favourite toy or comforter.
- Suffered a major change in their lives such as starting school, changing childminders, a new baby in the family, moving house etc.
- Experienced the death of a close family member.
- Experienced tension at home.
- Had a disagreement with a parent prior to being left; this can upset a child for the whole day until they see the parent again.
- Experienced the death of a pet.
- Fallen out with a friend.

The main thing child carers need to look for is a change in behaviour which is uncharacteristic for that particular child.

Children should be encouraged to explore and express their feelings in a variety of ways and you can encourage this by introducing suitable activities such as:

Emotional activities

Making masks

Provide the children with face templates and a variety of collage materials. Encourage them to make a face which reflects the way they are feeling. Talk to the child about how they are feeling and ask them whether they are happy, sad, worried or excited. Help children to understand that it is perfectly natural to have emotions.

Role play

This is an excellent way of encouraging children to explore their emotions. They should be allowed to use props in whatever context they wish in order to express their feelings.

Painting

Encourage the children to paint pictures of their life at home including the house they live in, their parents, siblings, pets etc.

Stories

Stories which encourage children to talk about their feelings are a useful way of exploring emotions and help children to realize that they are not alone in the way they feel. Select stories which cover common topics such as starting school, going into hospital or welcoming a new baby into the family.

Figure 5.1 Emotional activities

Growing Independence

There is a fine balance between safety and independence and, as a childminder, it is essential that you allow the children in your care the opportunity to develop their independence without ever compromising on their safety. Doing this is not always easy. Young children love to explore and as this is one of the main ways they learn you should not prevent them from doing so. Older children love to feel grown up and enjoy being given the responsibility of going to the shops or walking home from school alone. Never allow the children in your care this type of responsibility without prior written permission from their parents. It is important that children are educated from an early age about safety issues, without frightening them.

Encouraging self-help is a great way of allowing children to become independent. The more children can do for themselves the more self-reliant and confident they will become. Encourage children to dress themselves, wipe their own nose and wash and dry their own hands. Offer choices to the children and allow them to make mistakes and learn how to correct these themselves.

There will be times when you, the adult, will need to take a back seat and allow the children the opportunity to solve problems and work things out for themselves. They may well make mistakes but it is important that they are allowed to assess situations and undertake challenges without your help in order for them to develop their independence. Always be on hand to offer support, praise and encouragement. Adults need to show an enormous amount of patience in order to help children to take on responsibility and become self-reliant. Learning how to tie shoelaces or put on a coat, for example, will take dozens of attempts and you should avoid having too high an expectation of what the child can achieve because it will seriously undermine their confidence if you criticize their attempts or take over in order to speed up the pace. Always allow lots of time for the child to carry out the task at their own pace.

There are many everyday opportunities which could be used to encourage children to develop self-reliance and independence. Some of these are listed below:

- Offering the child choices.
- Encouraging the child to look after toys and equipment.
- Encouraging the child to carry out simple self-help tasks such as washing hands, wiping their own nose etc.
- Allowing the child to help with simple tasks such as preparing snacks or pouring drinks.
- Encouraging the child to put on their own shoes and coats.
- Encouraging the child to hang up their own coat.
- Asking the child to help tidy up after play.

Learning personal independence will allow the child to feel grown up and responsible. It is very tempting for an adult to do things for a child even if they do not need assistance, simply because it is quicker and easier; this will not benefit the child. Resist taking control and allow the child to enjoy the sense of achievement they will inevitably feel after they have put their own coat and shoes on ready for the journey to school.

Facing up to Fears

Almost every child will, at some point in their lives, develop a fear of something. It may be a fear of spiders, the dark, or thunder and lightening. Fortunately, childhood fears are usually mild and the child will quickly grow out of them.

There are two main types of fears:

Social fears

These are experienced when having to meet new people, give a talk or eat in public. Social fears are usually experienced by older children, probably between the ages of 10 and 12, when they are becoming more socially aware and feel the need to be accepted.

Specific fears

These are experienced when having to face certain things which cause anxiety, like spiders and the dark.

> **Exercise**
>
> What are you afraid of? Can you honestly say that nothing fazes you? How do you feel about visiting the dentist or doctor, for example? Would you happily climb a ladder or catch a spider? Make a list of some of the common things that may cause children to develop fears.

One of the most common fears in early childhood is the fear of separation. Children often have an irrational fear of being separated from their parents. Children who are new to your setting may well cry each time they are dropped off at your home, regardless of how much fun you manage to cram into their day! Separation fear is normal and is something that you should expect and be prepared for. It will usually only last for a short time and you can help the child to settle by giving them lots of reassurance and encouragement. Explain to the child that their parents will be back soon and reiterate how much fun they will have with you before their parents return. Providing a well-structured day will help a child who suffers from separation anxiety.

Although many children develop fears for no apparent reason, anxiety can also be learned from those around them. Sometimes it can be good for children to witness wariness in the adults around them so that they learn to respect objects which can hurt them, such as a hot oven or an iron, and learn the dangers of busy roads and sharp knives. However, at times parents and other adults can unwittingly 'teach' children how to react by exhibiting their own fears. Watch how you react to a spider or a mouse. If you shriek and run away you will be sending out the wrong message to a child who may be witnessing your behaviour. This type of negative response can have a strong influence on a child and they may well end up copying your behaviour, therefore developing an irrational fear.

Unfortunately some children simply have an anxious personality and are naturally fearful. If you are caring for a child with a fussy temperament try to ascertain why they appear so unsettled. This could be for a variety of reasons. They may have experienced disruption at home such as the death of a close relative, divorce or separation of their parents, an illness etc., or they may have experienced a lot of change in their lives resulting in a lack of security and reluctance to form friendships.

Very occasionally children may develop fears to the extent that they totally disrupt their lives, and simple tasks such as going outdoors can be tainted with a fear of what they may come across. If this is the case then it may be necessary to seek expert help and advice from a doctor or child psychologist. Always speak to the child's parents before seeking any outside help.

Important points to consider if you are caring for a child suffering from any type of fear or phobia:

- Always treat the fear with respect no matter how small it may appear to you. Never ridicule the child or undermine their fear.
- Seek parental advice. Talk to the parents about their child's behaviour and work out together how to tackle the problem effectively. It may be that one or both of the parents are unwittingly adding their own anxieties to their child's fear.
- Offer lots of reassurance.
- Encourage the child to face up to their fears. Avoiding the problem will not help the child to overcome their fears, in fact it may well add to the problem as the child will not develop the skills needed for them to cope. Offer support to the child when they come face to face with their fear and talk them through the experience in a calm manner. Never force a child to overcome their fears by having unrealistic expectations. A child who is afraid of spiders is not going to enjoy having half a dozen of them crawling all over their arms and it is not necessary for them to do so. It is quite sufficient for the child to be comfortable walking confidently past a spider's web.

Self-confidence and Self-esteem

It is important to understand that the way a child feels about themselves will affect the way they behave and relate to others. A child who has very little self-confidence and who is made to feel inadequate or stupid may well end up believing they are worthless and find it difficult to make friends, wrongly thinking that no-one will want to be their friend. Alternatively, a child who is full of confidence and who knows they are loved and wanted will probably have lots of friends and be happy to attempt new things.

Praise and encouragement therefore play a very important part in building self-esteem and confidence. Praise and encouragement can come from an adult in many forms and does not necessarily have to be simply the spoken word, although this is the simplest and most effective method of showing the children that you value their efforts and achievements. Other ways of encouraging children include:

- Displaying the child's work attractively on the walls.
- Providing the child with a special book or folder to keep their work in.
- Using reward charts.
- Issuing stickers and badges for effort and achievement.
- Issuing special certificates for effort and achievement. These need not be expensive, shop-bought ones; they can easily be produced on a computer.

Exercise

Design your own certificate which you could use in your setting to issue to children who have shown exceptional behaviour, been helpful or tried really hard.

It is important to remember that while some children relish the opportunity of developing their self-help skills and enjoy being able to do things for themselves, others may not. Some children attempt to tie shoelaces from a very young age, while others would happily allow an adult to carry out such tasks for them for many years. A child's willingness to do things for themselves and therefore develop independence may depend on several factors:

- How much encouragement they are getting. You, the childminder, may well be encouraging the child but what is the parents' attitude to independence?
- Developmental delays.
- The position of the child's place within the family. Older children tend to be more independent whereas younger siblings may be used to having their older brothers and sisters doing things for them.

Although children develop at different rates and it is important not to compare children's abilities, there are some milestones which you would do best to encourage children to reach before they start school in order to give them the independence and self-confidence they will need. Children around the age of five years should be able to:

- Dress themselves.
- Go the toilet independently and be able to clean themselves and wash their own hands appropriately.
- Recite their name and address.
- Be able to use the appropriate implements needed to feed themselves. These may be a knife, fork and spoon or chop sticks depending on the child's personal cultural upbringing.
- Be able to mix acceptably and play with others.

Incorporating ICT

ICT applications can be used successfully in emotional activities. A child who has a fear of spiders, for example, can be encouraged to use a computer in order to gain information about them. Often fear is bred by ignorance and the more information available to the child the better equipped they will become to deal with their fears. ICT applications offer a safe way of exploring and facing up to fears.

Useful Websites

Resources can be purchased from:

www.kidpremiership.com

   Books and learning resources

www.scholastic.co.uk

   Books and resources

www.tts-shopping.com

   Learning resources

Communication, Language and Literacy

6

Play is a very valuable tool for developing communication, language and literacy. Certainly, each new activity, learning experience or plaything will allow for the expansion of a child's vocabulary and it is important that adults introduce new words at every opportunity. Encourage the child to talk about what they are doing, what they can see, hear, feel and smell. Adults need to answer a child's questions, which can at times be constant, with honesty and precision and should also encourage the child to ask further questions.

There are four main areas of communication, language and literacy:

1 Speaking

2 Listening

3 Reading

4 Writing.

Communication begins initially with speaking and listening. These key areas are vital for a child because their ability to read and write will follow on from their ability to speak and listen. Language is not simply a talking skill. Language is about listening, interpreting, understanding and conveying messages. Children need to be in an environment where they hear language being used all the time. Adults need to talk to babies and young children – even if they are not able to answer appropriately – and they should be encouraged to join in conversation from a very young age. A baby starts to absorb words from birth onwards.

Language and literacy underpin all aspects of a child's life and learning ability. The Curriculum Guidance groups the Early Learning Goals for Communication and Language into six categories:

- Language for communication
- Language for thinking
- Linking sounds and letters
- Reading
- Writing
- Handwriting.

Although it is important for childcare practitioners to be aware of these areas, it is equally important to look at the development of the child as a whole and understand that this does not occur in individual phases, it overlaps. As a child develops in one area so too will they be improving in another, and often each skill will support and develop another. Communication, language and literacy are gradual learning skills which children achieve over a period of time. For example, a child does not go from being a non-reader one day to being a competent reader the next. Reading, like language and writing, is a skill which is developed over time.

Language and literacy activities are many and varied. However, it is important to remember that planned activities, though useful, should not replace simple, spontaneous conversations with the children. Childminders are often busy, rushing from playgroup, nursery and school to clubs, support groups etc. However, it is essential that you take the time simply to stop, listen and talk to the children. Spontaneous conversations are often the most valuable as they take into account what the child is doing at that time and what interests them the most.

Activities to Promote Communication, Language and Literacy

Storytelling boxes

These are very easy to make and will encourage a child's imagination. Using an old box, decorate it either by covering it with wrapping paper or wall paper or painting it (enlist the help of the children to do this with you). Put four or five objects in the box which you consider suitable to inspire a story. If you are particularly artistic you could make the box look like a house or a farm and add objects associated with them such as farm animals and a tractor. Allow the children time to explore the contents of the box and then listen to them as they begin to 'act out' their story using the box and its contents.

Role play

Children should be provided with suitable dressing-up clothes and props which enable them to take part in role play. Make-believe forms a very large part of a child's play and they often like to pretend to be teachers, doctors or air pilots. When helping the children to prepare the setting for a particular role play, encourage them to use props which promote literacy. For example when pretending to run a café or restaurant the children can make recipes and menu boards and be encouraged to take down orders on a note pad.

Name boards

Introduce a name board into your setting. This is a similar idea to 'signing in', but for young children who have not mastered the skill of writing, this activity encourages them to recognize the way their name looks when it is written down. Make a simple welcome notice and pin it to the wall. Write the children's names on pieces of card with blue tak or sticky tape on the back and encourage them to select their name tag and place it on the board.

Magnetic boards and letters

are a good way of encouraging children to recognize the 26 letters in the English alphabet (more if you count the various different capital letters as well!). Magnetic letters can be stuck on fridges and washing machines and children will enjoy using them to make up words.

Toy telephones

These toys are invaluable in the childminding setting as they encourage children to converse with one another while playing. Take the time to listen to the children while they pretend to talk on the telephone – quite often they say things which they have probably heard their parents say and it may sound very different to the way they usually talk.

Figure 6.1 Promoting communication, language and literacy

Linking Sounds and Letters

There are several gradual processes to language development. A child who starts to use language realizes, firstly, that sentences can be broken down into words. Secondly, they begin to realize that there are sounds within words.

As children get older, usually by around the time they reach their third birthday, they begin to realize that some words rhyme and that longer words have syllables.

It is debatable, when encouraging children to learn the alphabet, whether we should teach them the sound of the letter, the name of the letter, or indeed both. It can be argued that knowledge of letter sounds is more helpful to children initially, when they first begin to learn to read and write. However, teaching both letter sounds and names of letters can be confusing. It must be understood that a child is constantly developing their language skills. By allowing the child to listen to you and conversing together you will be encouraging these skills on a daily basis.

Books, rhymes and songs are an important way of expanding a child's vocabulary.

Reading

Reading is a hugely complex process which demands a wide network of knowledge and skills. The skill of reading is a gradual process which is acquired over a period of time.

Talking and listening to children from babyhood is the best preparation for reading that you can provide. One of the main strategies for learning to read comes from the child's ability to understand language through speaking and listening to adults and other children. Being unable to read and write is known as illiteracy and this is a serious disadvantage in many cultures. However, it is important to remember that not all cultures use the written word. The Celtic language has an oral culture and so too do the Maoris in New Zealand.

Reading is a gradual process and not one that is achieved overnight. There are several aspects to reading:

- Understanding the text
- Interpreting the text
- Enjoying the text
- Enjoying the pictures.

Children can be encouraged to look at words and pictures and to recognize letters.However, the speed at which they learn to read will vary with each individual. Being able to read largely depends on the child's ability to 'decode' the words. Before a child can become a confident reader it is necessary for them to master the skills involved in pre-reading such as:

- Learning how to handle books – knowing which way up to hold the book, how to turn pages and which page to look at first.
- Being aware that printed words have meanings.
- Learning how to use the pictures to predict storylines.
- Enjoying books, both looking at them alone and enjoying stories as a group.
- Having knowledge of nursery rhymes.

When talking about books for children we tend to think of them as purely story books or picture books. However, this is not the case, and there are a large selection of books on the market which are aimed at children:

- Picture books
- Story books
- Feely books – textured books using a variety of tactile materials, ideal for the very young or for children with sensory impairments
- Pop-up books
- Poetry books
- Nursery rhyme books
- Factual books.

Reading and looking at books are activities which can be enjoyed both alone and as a group and it is important that childcare practitioners encourage children to look at books. You can do this by ensuring that you have a good selection of books suitable for the age and stage of development of *all* of the children in your care. Make your quiet corner or reading area attractive and comfortable, with child friendly bookshelves which are easily accessible. Books get tatty very quickly and are easily torn, so you will need to replace them on a regular basis. Encourage children to handle books correctly to prolong their life, and teach them to understand that books are vital to learning and as such should be treated with respect.

Exercise

Look closely at the books you have in your own setting. Do you have suitable reading material for *all* the children in your care? If not, make a list of the books you need to buy and which ones you could borrow from your local library.

When reading with a child allow the child to turn the pages for you and take time to discuss the pictures as well as reading the text. A child who is unable to read can still be included in the reading activity by encouraging them to talk about what they can see in the pictures and to anticipate what they think will happen next.

0–3 Years

Children of all ages love books. However, it is important to provide books which are suitable for the age of the child in order for them to gain anything from them. Very young children should not be given books with paper pages as they will quickly become spoilt. Babies and young children put things in their mouths and books are no exception. Picture books with cardboard pages and bright illustrations, which are appealing to the eye, are ideal for this age group. Avoid lengthy text; even with an adult reading the story, young children will tire very quickly. Once a child has absorbed the picture they will be ready to turn the page! Feely books which use texture and sound are also very good for children of this age group.

3–5 Years

Children of this age group have usually begun to understand the meaning of books and recognize the words as well as the pictures. It is still very important to provide books which are visually inspiring because most children between the ages of 3 and 5 will not have learned how to read text. Activity books are particularly useful for this age range as they encourage the child to participate in the story. Look out for books which ask the reader to spot things within the pictures or which ask questions to encourage both reader and listener to take part in the activity.

5–7 Years

Children of this age are usually starting to learn how to read text and will bring home books from school. Quite often the books provided by schools are part of a series involving the same characters. These books encourage the child to recognize the characters and feel confident attempting new stories. The main problem with introducing children to set books which include the same characters is that they sometimes lack the confidence to attempt to read other books, assuming that if they do not include their known 'characters' they will be unable to read them. To combat this problem, ensure that you have sufficient books in your setting with a similar quantity of text to the books the child is bringing home from school. Let the children compare the books so that they can be sure in their own minds that the words may be different but that there is no reason why they shouldn't be able to read both. Once the child has gained confidence in their own reading ability they should begin to attempt to read different books and will have no difficulty in selecting a book for themselves from your bookshelves.

7–11 Years

Children of this age are beginning to understand the importance of books and realize that reading is an enjoyable learning activity. You should be introducing lengthier reading material with fewer and fewer pictures as the child gets older. It is a good idea to provide magazines and comics for the children to enjoy in addition to books. Children between the ages of 7 and 11 years are able to concentrate much longer on reading material and will often enjoy stories with more complex plots or action themes.

11–14 Years

By the time a child reaches the age of 11 years they should be confident readers, and while not all children will enjoy reading, they should be capable of reading and understanding a story which has no visual content. Younger children rely heavily on pictures to help and encourage them to read the words and will quite often guess at the text using the pictures as a reference. A child of 11 should be competent in reading text without pictures and, more importantly, be able to comprehend what they have read. Children of this age will understand the importance of books, not just for stories, but as reference and educational material and should be confident using a dictionary or encyclopaedia for assistance.

14–16 Years

By the time a child reaches the age of 14 they will have used text books to gain information on a regular basis both at school and at home. They will probably have read a large number of books and will most certainly have a preference for the type of books they like, whether these are romance, thriller or action. You should provide books which interest and inspire them in order to feed their imagination and continue their love of reading. A setting should have suitable reading material of interest to everyone. Although books can be expensive, many can also be bought at discounted prices from clearance shops and through the internet. Amazon, for example, offers many books at great savings. Libraries are another great source of accessing thousands of books free of charge, and children should be encouraged to join a library from a young age.

Writing

There are two important aspects which make up writing:

- Handwriting and letter shape – the way the writing looks.
- The meaning of the words – what the word actually 'says'.

Most languages are made up of a written 'code'. When children learn to read they learn to 'decode' the words; when they learn to write they learn to construct 'codes'.

Before a child successfully learns how to write words they will have been developing their skill through the drawing of symbols. Pictures and scribble are examples of how children begin to experiment with writing.

0–3 Years

Children between the ages of 0 and 3 rarely write words with any meaning. By the time they reach their third birthday some children have mastered some or all of the letters in their name; however, most of their writing is still illegible and will consist of various shapes intermingled with pictures which appear to have little resemblance to adult writing. Children should be encouraged without interference, and it should be understood that there is no real need for children of this age to be competent in writing skills. Young children should be allowed to experiment, perhaps by using techniques such as writing in a sand tray or in the air, using finger paints and using chalk on a blackboard.

3–5 Years

By the time a child gets to this age they should have mastered the fine motor skills associated with holding a pencil correctly. They should have determined which hand they are most comfortable writing with, though it is not uncommon for children to experiment writing with both their right and left hands. Never encourage a left-handed child to use their right hand. Allow children to see text in books and encourage them to seek out other forms of writing when you are out and about. Shop signs, road signs, car number plates, house names etc. are all examples of text which children can be encouraged to recognize and 'decode'.

5–7 Years

There is no set age for a child to master writing successfully; while some children can write their name at 3 years old, others may be well into their primary school education before they begin to form their letters successfully. Children should not be pushed into learning to write too young as this can have a detrimental effect later in their lives when they view writing as a chore and may even dislike the task. One of the most beneficial ways an adult can encourage and help a child with their writing skills is to point out letters and text and encourage the child to explore their own way of writing. Children between the ages of 5 and 7 often find it easier to write capital letters and they may begin to write using capital letters or a mixture of both capitals and lower case. Although children in the UK are often encouraged to begin taking part in formal writing exercises when they begin reception class, around the age of 4 or 5, many other countries do not expect children to learn to write until they reach the age of 6 or 7.

7–11 Years

By the time a child reaches the age of 7 years they will have begun formal handwriting lessons at school. Emphasis will be placed on the neatness of the handwriting and the child's ability to 'join up' the letters. Children are beginning to become competent writers by the age of 7 and should be able to produce written work which is legible and makes sense, although there may be a great number of spelling errors because children usually write words as they sound. By the time a child nears their eleventh year they should be more competent at spelling and should be knowledgeable about using a dictionary.

11–14 Years

By the time a child has reached the age of 11 years they should be competent and confident with their writing ability. They will be able to write lengthy pieces of text and use a variety of words to express themselves. Spelling may still be a problem for some because this is a skill which does not always come easily and must be practised. For children to learn to write stories it is essential that they explore different roles, characters and themes and, as a child carer, this is something that you should be encouraging.

14–16 Years

Young people of this age will usually have learned how to write confidently and competently. They should be happy producing both creative writing and academic pieces and should have mastered the art of neat, legible handwriting with correctly formed and joined letters.

English as an Additional Language

Today the United Kingdom is a culturally diverse country and, as such, it is more likely that children will learn more than one language. Children who are able to use two languages are *bilingual* and those who can use several languages are *multilingual*. The languages used may not just be of the spoken word, they may include sign language.

It is absolutely paramount, as a childcare practitioner, that you are aware of the context of the child's language ability and how it is being taught at home. For example, a child who is learning German from their father will not have the same language needs as a child who is hearing only Welsh from both his parents. A child who is learning two or more languages may be slightly slower in their language progress than those learning just one. However, with the correct support this delay should not affect their overall language development. It is widely believed that a child needs to be confident in their home language before they can become competent in others. As a childminder it is important that you respect the child's home language and work with their parents to establish a suitable, workable programme for the child. This could mean the child learning each language separately with a particular person, i.e. the home language with the parent and English with you, the childminder. Generally speaking, if you stick to your own language when talking to the child this will enable them to recognize which language is acceptable in which situation and you will prevent the child from becoming confused. The amount and quality of the adult support the child is shown will determine the speed at which the child's language develops.

Occasionally, children who use more than one language may have problems learning specific words in each language and therefore suffer gaps in their vocabulary. This may occur when a child plays with a particular toy or takes part in an activity which he or she would not normally have the opportunity to do at home. The child may then go home and try to tell their parents what they have done but find it difficult to source the correct words to describe the toy or activity in the home language. These problems can be overcome by talking to the parents yourself about their child's day and what they have done with you. Encourage the parents to come into your home and see what kind of activities you have available in order for them to be able to help their child describe what they have experienced.

Always make sure that bilingual and multilingual children have their additional languages recognized and valued in order for them to feel accepted. Cultural diversity should be recognized and celebrated. However, it is important to make sure that children who speak more than one language are not made to feel different or asked to 'perform' their language skills for others. Children may feel embarrassed or uncomfortable if asked to say 'hello' or 'thank you', for example, in their home language and you should never put a child in this kind of predicament. Likewise, accents are regarded as part of our cultural heritage and you should be sensitive to a child's regional and local accent. Never ridicule a child or make them feel different because of the way they speak.

Incorporating ICT

Children who have difficulties with writing can use a word processor to record their work successfully. Spelling and word correction facilities enable children with dyslexia to correct common mistakes, thereby developing their confidence. Allowing a child to use a computer to produce written work also eliminates the need for erasing mistakes or for teachers to have to correct large amounts of written work, which can often result in a child losing confidence in their ability. The computer's programs and correction facilities encourage children to find and amend the mistakes themselves.

Useful Websites

www.scholastic.co.uk

Books and resources

www.teacherstuff.org.uk

Ideas on teaching children

www.teachingideas.co.uk

Ideas on teaching children at Foundation Level

www.thebigbus.com

Interactive learning for 3–11 year olds

www.funwithspot.com

Ideas to promote literacy, numeracy and ICT skills

www.ghbooks.com/activity

Early education books

www.theideabox.com

Education and activity resources

www.kidpremiership.com

Books and learning resources

www.mape.org.uk

Education through ICT

www.kids-channel.co.uk

Fun educational ideas and online games

www.kidsdomain.com

Fun educational ideas and online games centred around themes

www.tts-shopping.com

Learning resources for children

Problem Solving, Reasoning and Numeracy

Problem Solving

Problem solving requires the ability to use logical thinking and apply mathematical skills in a practical situation.

Childminders should provide experiences which allow the children in their care to:

- Plan methods
- Give predictions
- Offer explanations.

Children take part in problem-solving situations on a daily basis through their play; for example, they may be building a track for the trains to run on and may need to work out how high the bridge will need to be in order for the train to pass underneath. Construction and creative play offer excellent sources for promoting problem solving and children will often achieve a solution to a problem they encounter. Although it is vital that children are allowed to work out solutions to problems themselves, it is also important that the adults around them offer support, help and advice when necessary. Childminders must work closely with the children, listen and observe them. It is important to ask open-ended questions to assist a child with problem solving rather than offer an outright answer. For example, a child who is struggling with a jigsaw puzzle should not be told where to fit the pieces but asked questions to help them solve the problem themselves; you might encourage the child to look closely at the shape and colour of a piece and encourage them to turn the piece around in order for it to fit.

Introducing Mathematics Including Shape, Measurements, Money and Time

As with many areas of learning, babies and young children begin to understand mathematics and scientific concepts from birth. These concepts enable a child to make sense of the world they live in and the things around them. Children should be allowed to explore their environment and offered support and encouragement. A good childcare practitioner recognizes when a child needs assistance and when to take a step back and allow the child to experiment for themselves, even if this means the child making mistakes. Firsthand experiences are essential in order for children to learn effectively.

Mathematics is based on everyday experiences. These experiences lead directly to an understanding of the relationships between things such as:

- Time
- Space
- Length
- Volume
- Capacity
- Shape
- Size
- Number
- Weight
- Pattern
- Area.

Mathematics involves problem solving and recording. It should have a meaning and function which children are able to link with their everyday lives.

Shape and Size

The key when introducing mathematical concepts to young children is not to complicate things. Avoid using difficult words and stick to general terms. Talk to the children about shapes and sizes while you are together and involve them in simple tasks such as putting the shopping away. Talk about the apples and carrots you have bought. Describe their size and shape. Introduce new words and teach the child opposites such as:

- Big and small
- Heavy and light
- Round and flat

- Long and short
- Fat and thin.

Additional mathematical concepts can then be introduced by encouraging the children to compare the objects and by talking about the apple being 'smaller than' or 'bigger than' another object.

Measurements

Measuring objects can be done in a variety of ways including:-

- Shape
- Size
- Weight
- Length
- Volume and capacity
- Area.

In order for children to appreciate each of these aspects of measurement they should be allowed to experience them for themselves and explore and experiment. For example, to fully understand the meaning of weight a child will need to feel for themselves whether something is heavy or light. Allow them to carry a bag of flour and then give them a feather to hold. Encourage them to talk about the differences. Provide weighing scales for them to use along with suitable substances for them the weigh.

When introducing length to young children it is best to avoid specific concepts such as centimetres, metres and miles. It is much better to describe the length of something to a child by using the words 'longer than' or 'shorter than'. You should provide children with measuring equipment such as rulers, tapes and height charts so that they become aware of how things are measured. However, it is best to allow them to understand gradually the concept of exact lengths.

Volume and capacity can be explored in ways that are often of interest to young children. Filling buckets, jars, jugs and bottles with water is usually an enjoyable activity for young children. Measuring jugs with fluid ounces, litres and pints marked on them are good for accurately reading capacity. However, like specific lengths, do not complicate the child's learning at a young age by dwelling on specific measurements; instead, talk about how the bucket is full or the bottle is almost empty.

Area can be described satisfactorily to children by using everyday items to describe it. For example, the table cloth covers the area of the table or the carpet covers the area of the floor. Area can also be explored when playing with building bricks or making models out of boxes and cartons.

Money

Children are often fascinated with money long before they have a true understanding of its value. They like to handle coins and often show an interest in having money of their own to spend. Children can be encouraged to explore the concept of money and why we use it by providing them with role play opportunities which explore buying and selling. Take the children shopping with you and allow them to choose something themselves, pay for it and wait for their change, explaining each process as you go along.

It is important that children learn the value of money and understand that different countries use different currencies.

Arrange to visit your bank with the children in your care and let them see how money is paid in or drawn out of your account. Talk to them about the facilities available in a bank such as cheque books and savings account pass books. If there is a 'Bureau de Change' within your bank, discuss with the children what this is for and reinforce this by showing them holiday brochures and foreign currency and talking about their own holiday experiences.

There are many activities which you could use within your setting to introduce children to money, such as arranging a treasure hunt. Hide coins in the sand tray and allow the children to dig for buried treasure! This activity could be extended for older children by adding objects to the sand tray and then making a treasure map so that the children can follow instructions in order to find the treasure. Encourage the children to roll coins and see which coins roll the furthest. Look at the shape and size of the coins and talk about the value of each.

Children should be encouraged to explore other ways in which things can be purchased which may not involve the exchanging of cash, such as using credit cards and cheques.

Time

It is not always easy for young children to comprehend the true meaning of time; quite often, for example, they have little idea of how long they have spent on a particular activity. If they are enjoying what they are doing they may well spend a lot of time carrying out the task, whereas if they are bored they may flit from one activity to another relatively quickly. Try asking a young child what they did yesterday and you will probably get a very different answer from their response to being asked what they did last Tuesday! Young children may well remember what they did on holiday three months ago but find it hard to tell you what they did only a couple of days ago. This is because the time spent on holiday was different and enjoyable, whereas what they did the other day may be routine and, to the child, rather boring.

By the time a child reaches the age of 4 years they can usually understand what is meant by the words yesterday, today and tomorrow, although they may still be unable to recall what they have done throughout the course of a full week.

Time is an abstract concept and it is not usually until a child reaches their second year of full-time school that they begin to understand how time is measured. It is possible to encourage children to understand the notion of time by referring to events in the day such as 'after lunch' or 'it's time to tidy up'.

Time can be explored in an enjoyable way through the use of time pieces, particularly those which chime or have special features, for example a cuckoo clock.

Numeracy Activities

Dominoes

This encourages children to recognize numbers and improve addition skills.

Bingo

This encourages children to recognize numbers. This traditional game can be extended by making your own bingo cards depicting mathematical sums. The 'caller' then pulls numbers out at random and the players cover their sums when the correct answer has been called.

Eg. 3×6

$12 - 4$

These sums would be covered when the numbers 18 and 8 are called respectively.

Snakes and ladders

Another good game to encourage children to add up and recognize numbers and learn about sequences.

Simple card games

These encourage number recognition and numeracy skills.

Figure 7.1 Numeracy activities

Incorporating ICT

ICT can be successfully used to encourage children to learn about problem solving, reasoning and numeracy. For example, young children are fascinated to learn about the moon and the planets and ICT can be used to encourage them to find out about the solar system and time travel.

Using the internet to source information about length, height, weight and volume is both fun and interesting for children and they can be encouraged to print off a measurement chart to keep track of certain areas of growth such as height and weight.

Useful Websites

www.thebigbus.com

A range of online activities involving numbers

www.allparents.co.uk

A range of interesting ideas for numeracy activities

Knowledge and Understanding of the World

Knowledge and understanding of the world is the area of learning where children develop the skills which will help them to make sense of the world around them. It is important that childminders offer children a wide range of experiences which will help them to develop these skills. Children are naturally curious and will be in awe the first time they discover something for themselves. Encourage their willingness to learn by joining in with their enjoyment of the wonder of their surroundings and by asking appropriate questions and encouraging the children to do the same. You may have seen hundreds of rainbows in your lifetime but when a young child sees one for the first time they will be curious and want to explore. Extend and encourage their curiosity by allowing the children to paint their own rainbows and experiment with water. Provide information for the child, using books and the internet, and talk about the discovery in detail. Allow the children the opportunity to make their own rainbows by placing a jar of water on a sunny window ledge and see what happens. Experiment using prisms and expand on the activity to include shadows and shades of colour.

Although curiosity is natural in children and allows them to explore, often without fear, they must also learn how to do their exploring in a logical and systematic way. Children need to think things through, to anticipate the outcome and consider the implications of their actions. When using a computer for the first time, for example, many children will press every button on the keyboard regardless of what may happen. They should, however, be encouraged to consider their actions as they may of course lose data or break the machine with haphazard explorations. Remember that children need to do things for themselves and they will learn much more through firsthand experiences which allow them to become involved in the activity.

Knowledge and understanding of the world can be divided into two key areas of learning:

- The scientific and technological aspects of both the natural and man-made world.
- The historical, human, social, geographical and environmental aspects of people, places, time and space.

A sensory approach to introducing children to the world should be adopted, encouraging children to touch, smell, listen and observe the things around them. Young children should not, however, be encouraged to taste unfamiliar substances without supervision as there are inherent dangers involved. The sense of taste can of course be explored under adult supervision, for example during cooking activities.

Intellectual activities to promote knowledge and understanding of the world in young children should encourage them to:

- Ask questions critical to their thinking –

  What is this?
  Where is this?
  Who is this?
  Why is this?

- Use their powers of understanding through their senses.
- Recognize objects through using their senses.
- Recognize shapes, colours and patterns.
- Understand mathematical processes and be able to arrange, sort and categorize objects into groups.
- Recognize the properties of some materials and know the difference between soft and hard, rough and smooth or wet and dry.
- Understand the importance of time.
- Understand the seasons and changes in weather.
- Be able to care for living objects such as plants and pets.
- Identify and be confident using numbers up to ten when carrying out games and play experiences.
- Recognize shapes and be able to use mathematical language appropriate to the situation.
- Understand the everyday use of technology such as scissors, oven, fridge, washing machine etc.

Science and Technology

Science and technology are playing an increasingly complex part in our world today. Most of the changes which have come about during the past 100 years or so have been of great benefit. Illnesses, for example, which were once life threatening can now often be cured with antibiotics. Transport has revolutionized the way we travel, and simple domestic appliances, which we now take for granted, have enabled us to simplify our lives significantly. Not so long ago women spent all day doing the laundry using a wash tub and mangle whereas today we simply load a machine, press a button and walk away.

Science in the early years is all about the way we think rather than about complex experiments which need expert knowledge. The important thing to remember when planning a science activity for young children is to make sure that the activity encourages the children to question the world around them by:

- Observing
- Exploring
- Predicting
- Concluding.

Observing

Most children like to be involved 'hands on' in an activity, and this is by far the best way of holding their interest. However, they should also understand the importance of learning through observation. Adults should encourage the children to ask appropriate questions during the observation.

Exploring

Children should be encouraged to explore objects using their appropriate senses.

Predicting

Children should be encouraged to think about what might happen during a particular activity. For example, during a baking activity you could ask the children what they think will happen when the cake mixture is put into the oven or when the bread dough is put in a warm place. Predictions are not always easy for children, particularly if they are experiencing an activity for the first time. However wild their predictions, always value their answer and encourage them to take part.

Concluding

This is the part of the experiment when every part of the activity is taken into account. Talk about the experiment as a whole and discuss the predictions against the conclusion.

Consider the initial aim of the experiment and ask the children whether they have achieved what they set out to do. Ask questions like:

- What have we found out from this experiment?
- Did we guess the conclusion correctly?
- How can we remember what we have done?
- Could we have done things differently?
- Could we improve on the way we have done things?

Science Activities

Baking

Make a cake or some buns with the children. Allow the children to add the ingredients and talk about the way the mixture changes when certain things are added. Discuss, for example, the difference when egg is added and then flour. Encourage the children to predict what will happen to the cake if:

1. They put it in the oven.
2. They don't put it in the oven.
3. They leave it in the oven for too long.
4. They don't leave it in the oven for long enough.

Allow the children to taste the mixture throughout the activity and let them describe the smell, taste and texture of the cake mixture during the different stages. How different is the finished product in terms of the way it looks, smells and tastes?

Water

Experimenting with water is an excellent way of introducing science concepts to young children. Talk about water and its uses and importance. Provide opportunities for the children to freeze water by making ice cubes or ice lollies. Allow the children to make the mixture of juice and water and pour it into moulds. Encourage the children to predict what would happen if:

1. They put the mixture in the fridge.
2. They put the mixture in the freezer.
3. They leave the mixture on the table.

Encourage the children to check out how long the ice lollies take to freeze. Would they set quicker if hot water was used instead of cold? What happens to the lollies if they are taken out of the freezer once they are frozen? How long do they take before they melt?

Experiment with ice cubes:

How long do ice cubes take to set?

Do smaller cubes set quicker than larger ones?

What happens to the ice cube if you put it in cold water?

What happens to the ice cube if you put it in hot water?

Do the ice cubes float or sink?

Jelly

Allow the children to dissolve the jelly cubes in water, mix and pour into moulds. Talk about the texture of the jelly mixture and encourage the children to predict what will happen when the mixture is placed in the fridge. After the jelly has set, allow the children to touch it, wobble it and taste it.

Plants

Growing plants from seed is a good way of encouraging children to explore nature and learn about the importance of caring for living things. They will learn how sunlight and moisture play an important part in growth. Choose easy to grow seeds such as sunflowers which have a high success rate. Experiment with the seeds:

1. Allow the children to plant the seeds in separate pots.
2. Encourage the children to water some of the seeds but not all of them.
3. Place some of the seeds in direct sunlight and some in a dark cupboard.

Encourage the children to predict the growth of the seeds. How do their predictions compare with the seeds' actual growth?

Figure 8.1 Ideas for science activities

Intellectual Activities

Number concepts

Many everyday opportunities arise which are ideal for exploring number with young children. Setting the table, looking at numbers while out and about, for example on car registration plates and house doors, counting steps while climbing up or going down them, and singing songs and nursery rhymes will all encourage children to grasp number concepts.

Pattern

Jigsaw puzzles are an ideal way of introducing pattern to young children. More complex puzzles can be introduced once the child has gained confidence. Threading beads and simple sewing activities are also excellent ways of introducing pattern.

Shape

Provide the children with the opportunity to make models from junk materials. Egg boxes, cardboard boxes, tubes and yoghurt cartons hold an endless fascination for young children, who will turn them into works of art! Construction sets, building bricks and modelling materials such as plasticine and play dough are also useful materials for exploring shape.

Speed

Talk to the children about the way they move, whether they are walking, running, hopping or jumping, whether they are going slowly or quickly. Provide bicycles and other ride-on toys for children to experiment with.

Temperature

Baking and cooking activities are excellent for exploring the concept of temperature. Use the opportunity to talk about what happens to food when it is heated up or cooled down. Look at the seasons and talk about the weather both in this country and abroad. Which countries are hotter than ours and which are colder? Talk about the seasons and look at the different types of clothing worn at different times of the year.

Magnets

Children love to experiment with magnets. Provide magnets of different shapes and sizes and allow the children to work out which materials are attracted to the magnet and which are repelled.

Wormery

A wonderful way of introducing children to nature is by creating a wormery. This can be done relatively easily with a Perspex fish tank and soil. The children will enjoy seeing how the worms move around the tank and looking at the tracks left by their bodies.

Recycling

Encourage the children to get involved with recycling. Everyone should be aware of the necessity for recycling produce and you can help children to become environmentally aware by teaching them which products can be recycled and which cannot. Visit a bottle bank with the children and talk about how paper, clothing, organic material, plastic, glass and metal can be reused.

Science trays

Introduce science trays to your setting to enable the children to explore things such as texture, colour and sound. A science tray for texture could include a smooth pebble, fine and rough sandpaper, a nail file etc., whereas a science tray to introduce colour could include a torch, kaleidoscope, cellophane sweet wrappers, prisms scopes etc.

Figure 8.2 Ideas for intellectual activities

Cooking

Cooking and baking are excellent ways of introducing science to young children. Avoid complicated recipes which need lots of ingredients or elaborate cooking methods. Simple, quick recipes which require little or no cooking time are best suited to young children, who will find it difficult to concentrate on this type of activity for probably more than half an hour.

Suitable things to consider include:

1 Buns or cakes which can be mixed in one bowl. Allow the children to weigh, add and mix the ingredients. Think about how you are going to decorate the buns or cake, as this is one of the most enjoyable aspects of baking for the child. Coloured icing, cherries, chocolate and sugar strands are all suitable. Encourage the children to add food colouring to the icing and allow them to experiment.

2 Fruit salad is another easy recipe which requires no cooking. The children can explore a variety of fruits. Add exotic fruits such as kiwi and mango alongside the more popular apples, pears and bananas. Take the opportunity to look closely at the fruits whilst peeling and preparing them and talk to the children about the way the fruits change once they are peeled. For example, what happens to a banana when the skin has been removed? Encourage the children to look at the skins, cores and pips.

3 Chocolate Krispie buns – Rice Krispies or cornflakes mixed together with chocolate, placed in paper cases and left in the fridge to set are a no-cook alternative to traditional buns. Encourage the children to talk about the way the chocolate changes in appearance when it melts, and look at the way it binds the cornflakes together when mixed.

A Sense of Time

Many children find measuring time a difficult concept to understand. Often children are in their second year of primary school before they can fully understand how time is measured. As time cannot be 'seen' it is difficult for young children to comprehend the passing of time. Usually by the age of 4 or 5 years a child will understand the terms 'yesterday', 'today' and 'tomorrow'. However, it is unlikely they will be able to understand time in seconds, minutes or hours. Telling a child that their mum will be back in an hour or at half past four, for example, is meaningless to a young child.

Exercise

Think about how time appears to pass more slowly or quickly depending on what you are doing. Make a list of the situations you have encountered when time appeared to pass quickly and when it seemed to go slowly. Why do you think this happened? How many times have you looked at the clock today and thought the day has dragged? Do you often look at your watch and wonder where the time has gone?

Encourage the children in your setting to become aware of the concept of time by using appropriate language such as:

- Hour, minute, second.
- Day, week, month, year.
- Yesterday, today, tomorrow.

Talk about special occasions such as Christmas, birthdays and other festivals to allow children to anticipate their arrival and to be aware of the passing of time. Consider having a 'fun' clock in your setting which the children will enjoy looking at; this may have the face of a clown or an animal, for example. Chiming clocks and cuckoo clocks are also a good way of encouraging young children to become interested in time. Clock faces which allow the children to move the hands themselves can be purchased cheaply.

Time Activities

Clock faces

Make your own clock faces with the children using a piece of card or a paper plate. Add numbers and attach the hands with a clip so that they can be moved around the face.

Games

Incorporate games such as 'What time is it, Mr. Wolf?' or sing nursery rhymes which explore the concept of time such as 'Hickory, Dickory Dock'.

Festivals

Use festivals to show that certain times of the year are special, such as Easter, Christmas, Diwali, birthdays etc.

Charts/planners

Use charts or planners displayed on the wall to show important dates such as the children's birthdays, the first day of school, holidays etc. and encourage the children to count down the days to these events.

Calendars

Invest in a wall calendar which the children can be encouraged to change every day. There are many suitable calendars on the market and one which shows the day and date along with spaces to record the weather and special occasions is particularly appropriate for young children. Allow the children to take it in turns to change the calendar every day.

Seasons

Encourage the children to talk about the changing seasons and plan your activities accordingly. Picnics and obstacle courses in the summer, nature walks in the autumn and sledging in the winter, for example.

Time of day

Take the opportunity to incorporate time into your everyday routines. Tell the children it is almost lunch *time*, *time* to collect the older children from school, *time* for a nap, story *time* or home *time*.

Egg timers

Use egg timers instead of clocks to indicate the passage of time for younger children. Make it fun for the children by incorporating games into their learning. How many building bricks can you pick up before the sand runs out?

Past and present

Books, toys and clothing are excellent ways of introducing the passage of time to children. Toys which their parents and grandparents played with hold an endless fascination for young children. Clothes worn years ago can be used to talk about the differences in the way we dress today. Children are also intrigued by looking at the clothes they themselves wore as a baby and to see how they have grown since wearing them.

Figure 8.3 Ideas for time activities

Exercise

Make enquiries at museums near you to see what exhibitions or displays are available that may be of interest to the children. Often museums exhibit clothing and toys from past eras which may be suitable for the children in your care. Older children would benefit from a trip to a museum during the school holidays.

Incorporating ICT

ICT can be a very useful tool for expanding on a child's knowledge and understanding of the world, and the internet, when used appropriately, can open up a whole new and exciting world of learning. Limit the time the children are allowed to use the computer and encourage them to explore the world around them in other ways initially. It is more appropriate to conduct an experiment with the children in the first instance and then allow them to observe, explore, predict and conclude the outcome for themselves *before* encouraging them to use the computer for information. After the experiment or activity is complete, then the children should be allowed to find out more about what they have done, perhaps by using the computer and the internet. The computer is then being used as a tool to aid an experiment instead of being allowed to take the place of the experiment.

Consider using remote programmable toys such as racing cars and trains which allow the child to be active and practical in their learning. Speed, for example, can be explored in this way by using two cars racing around a track.

> **Exercise**
>
> Source a selection of programmable toys which could be useful in allowing children to be active in their learning.

Digital cameras are an excellent piece of equipment in an early years setting. These cameras allow the child to see their photograph instantly rather than having to wait for the film to be developed as with conventional cameras. Allow the children to take some photographs themselves. Always make sure that you have written parental permission prior to taking any photographs of the children in your care.

Useful Websites

www.ltl.org.uk
Learning Through Landscapes
www.thrive.org.uk
Thrive
www.gonegardening.com
Gone Gardening

Physical Development and Activities

9

The Importance of Fresh Air and Exercise

It is very important for children to have some form of exercise every day. Physical activity helps children to develop strength, become mentally alert and stay healthy.

In today's society, when the lifestyles of many children allow far less opportunity for physical exercise than in the past, it is vital that adults recognize the need to plan for physical activity. Not so very long ago most children had to walk to and from school; nowadays, however, the majority of children travel to school by car or bus, eliminating this chance for exercise.

Exercise in the early years should be fun and enjoyable. Children need space to run, stretch and explore, and whilst space can be limited indoors, gardens, parks, playgrounds etc. can provide excellent opportunities for children to exercise outside. Outdoor play and exercise should be encouraged all year round and can be enjoyed whatever the weather, providing children are dressed appropriately.

Physical exercise benefits children in a number of ways:

- It improves balance
- It improves coordination
- It improves flexibility
- It strengthens muscles
- It strengthens joints
- It improves appetite

- It increases bone density
- It increases blood circulation
- It develops strength and stamina
- It develops lung capacity
- It helps the digestive process.

All of these benefits give the child a feeling of well-being and also encourage interaction and cooperation.

It is important that adults make sure that children are aware of the effects that exercise can have on the body and that they are prepared to set aside times for rest during activities. This can be a good opportunity to talk to the children about how they feel before, during and after a vigorous exercise routine.

Exercise

Ask the children how they feel *before* they begin to exercise and then again *after* they have exercised. Do they notice a difference in:

- The way they are breathing?
- The temperature of their bodies?
- How tired they feel?

Encouraging children to understand the importance of regular exercise and how it benefits the body will help them to develop positive attitudes towards a sensible fitness routine.

Making Exercise Fun

When we talk about physical development we automatically think of exercise and outdoor play, but 'physical' exercise covers much more than just gross motor skills. Physical development covers the whole of the body and exercise is about how children learn to control every part of their body, including:

- ## Gross motor skills
  Movements which involve the arms and legs such as throwing and kicking a ball.

- Fine motor skills

  Small movements involving the whole of the hand such as catching a ball. Fine manipulative skills may also fall into this category and these involve controlling a pencil when learning to write or draw.

- Coordination skills

  This involves the ability to combine two or more skills at the same time. Coordinating the eye and foot, for example, while negotiating stairs, or using the hand and eye when building with bricks or threading beads.

- Balance

  Closely linked with coordination. Children learn how to control their bodies whilst riding a bike, for example, or walking in a straight line.

- Locomotive skills

  These skills involve controlling how the child runs, jumps and walks.

It is absolutely vital that children enjoy exercise. Expecting too much from them at the start or pushing them too far may put them off exercise and could potentially damage their opinion of exercise in the long term. Allow the children to explore at their own pace and to do only what they are happy and confident doing. Avoid over-encouragement and never 'goad' them into trying something for which they are not ready. In addition to this being dangerous, they may also lose confidence if they are unable to carry out a certain task.

Indoor Physical Play

It is probably true to say that the most vigorous activity will take place outdoors. However, it is important that child carers encourage both gross and fine motor skills indoors as well as out. It should be relatively easy for most childminding settings to incorporate indoor physical play.

Exercise

Think about how you can make sufficient space within your own setting in order to enable the children to enjoy indoor physical exercise. Push back a table, for example, roll up the rug and create a space which the children can use to enjoy physical exercise.

Dance, drama, active games, action rhymes and indoor obstacle courses are excellent ways of helping children to develop an awareness of how their bodies work while making the process fun and enjoyable.

Most children enjoy dancing and this can be done either through listening to music and moving freely or by building up set dance steps and routines which the children can learn. Encourage the children to select their own music and allow them to have a say in how the dance routine takes shape.

Drama can be used to extend other work and most children will enjoy acting out their favourite story. Older children can use drama as an extension of the setting's theme, for example learning about Easter could be developed into a play and extended to incorporate an Easter egg hunt.

Action rhymes can be enjoyed from a very young age and most children will quickly learn the actions to repetitive rhymes such as 'Old MacDonald had a Farm'. Actions can be incorporated to relate to the words and extended or simplified depending on the age and understanding of the child. Teach the children how to march and let them create their own marching band. Songs with actions are a very enjoyable way of incorporating exercise. Consider songs such as:

- Ring a Ring O'Roses
- The Farmer's in his Den
- The Grand Old Duke of York

- If You're Happy and You Know It (stamp your feet, clap your hands etc.)
- The Hokey-Cokey
- Oranges and Lemons
- Row, Row, Row your Boat.

Dancing is a fantastic way of introducing new cultures to the setting by allowing the children to explore the dances enjoyed in different countries.

- Ireland: traditional Irish dancing focuses on leg and feet movements whilst the hands and arms are held quite stiffly by the side.
- Spain: Spanish flamenco dancing involves lots of fancy footwork together with swinging hands and arms.
- India: Indian dancing is very lively and energetic. It involves lots of hand, arm, finger and head movements.
- Disco: encourage the children to have their own disco. Categories for the best slow dance, fast dance, dance sequence etc., can be organized.
- Ballet: A great way of encouraging balance and coordination. Introduce leotards and tutus to your dressing-up box.

Provide lots of colourful materials and dressing-up clothes to allow the children to experiment with the traditional costumes to complement each dance. Flowing skirts, saris, brightly coloured waistcoats etc., all make excellent dressing-up clothes.

> **Exercise**
>
> Make a list of all the songs you know which could have actions made for them. If you don't know the traditional actions make up your own. Remember to bear in mind the age and stage of development of the children in your particular setting and ensure that the actions you choose are suitable.

Active games are another great way of encouraging children to participate in indoor exercise. Consider introducing games such as:

- Simon Says
- Musical Chairs
- Musical Statues
- Follow My Leader
- Blind Man's Bluff.

Games such as Twister and Globe Trotting are fun to play and encourage exercise. These types of games require the child to stretch in order to place certain parts of their bodies on certain areas of a mat according to the instructions on the dial. For example, Globe Trotting may require the participant to place their right hand on Europe while their left leg may be in North America! Dance mats are also an excellent source of exercise.

You may like to consider making an indoor obstacle course. This could be very similar to the obstacle course you make outside but perhaps substitute soft foam balls or bean bags for footballs to avoid damage to furniture and furnishings.

It is possible to purchase various resources such as crazy golf and skittles which can be used just as effectively indoors as out. These resources are usually made of soft materials which are ideal for indoor use.

Outdoor Physical Exercise

It is perhaps much easier to think of ways for children to take part in physical exercise outdoors as space is not limited. There are many different games that children can take part in, such as traditional ball games:

- Football
- Cricket
- Rugby
- Tennis
- Golf.

Other team games, such as 'Tug of War' are ideal for outdoor play. Taking part in these sports will, however, depend on the age of the child and their ability to understand the rules. The games can, however, be simplified for young children by allowing them to kick, throw and hit a ball.

An outdoor obstacle course using hoops, balls, cones, skittles, skipping ropes and bean bags is an excellent way of incorporating outdoor physical exercise and this will encourage a variety of skills including balance and coordination. The course can be altered and extended as the child's ability progresses.

Ride-on toys, bicycles, tricycles, toy cars and other vehicles are another good source of exercise and these will strengthen the legs and improve balance. Fix stabilizers to bicycles initially and remove them once the child has gained sufficient balance.

Sand and water play is probably better suited to outdoors due to the amount of mess it inevitably creates. Children love to experiment with sand and water and this is an excellent way of improving fine motor skills by building sandcastles, sieving the sand, mixing sand with water etc.

Not all outdoor activity needs to take place in the garden. In fact, in some cases childminders may not actually have a garden or outdoor area for the children to enjoy. If this is the case then it is essential that you consider other ways in which the children can enjoy outdoor play and exercise. It is vital that you incorporate visits to the local playground or park into your routine and ensure that the children get regular opportunities for outdoor play and exercise. Although walking is a good source of exercise, children need the chance to run around and explore open areas such as parks and playgrounds in addition to walking.

Safety Tips

- Always supervise activities carefully.
- Take a basic first aid kit with you whilst out and about.
- If you take the children to a park or playground, check the area carefully for broken glass, dangerous debris or animal faeces.
- Ensure the children are dressed appropriately for the weather, with sun hats, cream etc., in hot weather and waterproofs in wet weather.
- Never use a finishing tape for races or obstacle courses. These are unnecessary and potentially dangerous as children can get caught up in them and choke.
- Bear in mind how hot children can get when running around, particularly in the summer. Try to avoid outdoor play at mid-day when the sun is at its hottest. Plan outdoor activities for morning or late afternoon and ensure you have plenty of refreshments available.
- Never push a child too far. Young children get tired quickly when running around and you should be careful not to allow them to get overtired. Take your cue from the children – when they have had enough, finish the activity.

Incorporating ICT

ICT does not just involve the use of computers. Tape recorders and CD players are all part of ICT and this type of equipment is invaluable when incorporating physical activities into your setting. Allow the children the opportunity to choose the type of music they enjoy and encourage them to bring CDs and tapes from home to share with the other children.

Music programs for the computer and sports websites are also excellent ways of introducing physical activities into your setting.

Useful Websites

www.elc.co.uk
 Indoor and outdoor resources can be purchased from Early Learning Centre

www.toysrus.co.uk
 Toys 'R' Us

www.earlyyearsresources.co.uk
 Early Years Resources

More sporty ideas can be found by visiting

www.youthsporttrust.org

www.bbc.co.uk/sportacademy

www.atozkidsstuff.com/oly.html

Creative Development and Activities

Feeding the Imagination

The use of the imagination is vital in order for children to play creatively. However, unlike mathematics and scientific concepts, imagination and creativity cannot be taught in the same way. In the early stages of their development, a child's imagination will be stimulated by what they see around them. Children need to be encouraged to use their imagination and this can be done in a variety of ways including:

- Allowing them plenty of time to play and explore. Avoid organizing the day too strictly or providing too many adult-led activities.
- Encouraging spontaneous play.
- Providing a wide range of materials for the children to use and explore in a variety of ways.

The more varied and exciting the child's experiences the more chances they will have of feeding their imagination.

Painting

Children should be offered frequent opportunities to paint. Painting is an invaluable way of allowing children to express themselves and will encourage the development of fine motor skills. Painting can be enjoyed by children of all ages and even very young children, who lack the skills of speech, can express themselves with spontaneous painting activities. Avoid questioning the child about their painting or commenting on how they can improve or add to their work. An adult's interpretation of a child's painting is often wrong and you should therefore avoid 'guessing' what the picture is unless invited by the child to do so. Children's confidence and self-esteem can take a huge battering if you jump in enthusiastically saying what you think of their beautiful flower when in fact they have painted a house!

During certain stages of a child's development it is perfectly normal for them to paint pictures using just one colour, very dark colours or all black paints. Do not assume that by painting in this way the child is trying to tell you that something awful has happened to them. Although some psychologists would have a field day, painting pictures in this manner is a natural progression of a child's development. Painting offers a child an excellent way of expressing their emotions and encourages imagination and creativity.

Painting Activities

- Butterfly painting: paint one side of a piece of paper. Fold the paper in half, press down and let the pattern transfer to the other side.
- Oil painting.
- Marble painting.
- Straw painting.

Figure 10.1 Ideas for painting activities

Exercise

Consider taking the children on a visit to an art exhibition or gallery. Talk about the paintings on display and ask the children which painting they liked the most and the least.

Drawing

In much the same way as painting, drawing offers an excellent opportunity for developing a child's imagination and fine motor skills. Drawing is central to all art and craft activities and encourages the child to explore pattern creation and builds on mathematical development. Drawing, like painting, helps to develop an awareness of composition, shape and colour and is an excellent activity for promoting anti-discriminatory practice, because both drawing and painting are essentially culture- and gender-free activities which can be enjoyed equally by all children.

Drawing Activities

- Wax crayon drawings.
- Pencil crayon drawings.
- Chalk drawings.
- Charcoal drawings.
- Felt tip pens and ink drawings.
- Coin/leaf/bark rubbings.

Figure 10.2 Ideas for drawing activities

Exercise

Consider making a special book for the children to put their drawings in or display them attractively on the wall of your setting.

Exercise

Look at the painting and drawing materials you provide and make sure that these resources allow children from all ethnic groups to represent themselves and their families realistically. Think about the colour of the paper you have provided and whether or not you have crayons and paints which include variations for skin tones. Do you have a selection of fluorescent materials, tactile tools, stubby brushes etc., which would enable a child with a sensory impairment or disability to enjoy the activity alongside others?

Printing

Printing, unlike painting and drawing, is a more structured form of creative design because the finished product will depend largely on the materials used rather than on the child's imagination and skill. Often children who are unhappy with the free expression needed for painting and drawing, or who may have less confidence, will be happier creating art forms from printing because they can use materials to help them create their art work. Printing is one of the best ways of introducing pattern to a child.

Printing Activities

- Use print pads or paint for hand and foot prints.
- Cut fruit and vegetables into shapes to use for printing.
- Use different materials to print with, such as sponges, rollers and string.
- Print with leaves and coins.
- Use toys and materials around the home to print with, such as Lego bricks, stickle bricks, keys and shells.
- Use objects from around the house such as cotton reels, hair combs, etc. to make patterns.

Figure 10.3 Ideas for printing activities

Collages

Making pictures out of collage materials is an excellent way for children to explore a variety of materials while creating a piece of art work. Children can use their imagination either to make a specific picture or, if the child is very young, to create patterns. Collage is a very versatile activity which uses a number of arts and craft based skills. The word 'collage' comes from the French word 'coller' which means 'to stick'. The main focus of collage work is cutting and sticking. Once children have mastered how to cut they can begin to create their own shapes for collage.

Collage Activities

Consider using the following materials for collage:

- A variety of paper such as tissue, crepe, foil.
- Pictures from magazines, holiday brochures etc.
- Pieces of fabric and felt.
- Shells and sand.
- Leaves, twigs, bark, wood shavings, acorns, seeds etc.
- Pasta, rice and pulses.

It is important that you consider the age and stage of development of the children in your care before providing certain materials. Small objects such as seeds, acorns etc., should not be given to very small children as they pose a threat of choking or injury if inserted in the ears or nose. Always take care when choosing which materials to provide for activities.

Figure 10.4 Ideas for collage activities

Model making

Junk modelling is a well-loved activity and many young children express themselves well when provided with an array of materials for modelling. Spaceships, rockets, boats, cars, towers and aeroplanes are among some of the objects children can create with a little imagination and plenty of recyclable materials. Modelling is a very 'hands on' craft activity which is full of possibilities for children of all ages. Modelling is an important way of introducing three-dimensional forms to a child in addition to exploring the art of cutting, sticking and decorating.

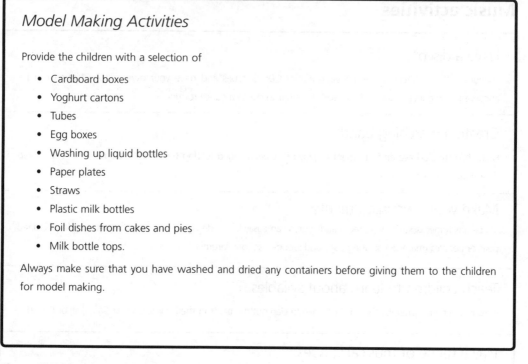

Model Making Activities

Provide the children with a selection of

- Cardboard boxes
- Yoghurt cartons
- Tubes
- Egg boxes
- Washing up liquid bottles
- Paper plates
- Straws
- Plastic milk bottles
- Foil dishes from cakes and pies
- Milk bottle tops.

Always make sure that you have washed and dried any containers before giving them to the children for model making.

Figure 10.5 Ideas for model making activities

Model making does not just involve making things out of 'junk'; it also includes the use of a variety of other materials such as play dough, clay, bread dough, plasticine etc.

Music

Music is an important part of a child's development and even from a very early age children will listen and respond to the sound of music. Have you ever observed a young baby while music is being played? They will often sway to familiar sounds! Many children love to listen and dance to music; however, it is equally important that they are encouraged to make music themselves either by using shop-bought instruments or by making their own. Music also provides an invaluable opportunity to spot possible impairments such as hearing loss, be this temporary or permanent.

Music activities

Have a disco

Encourage the children to bring their favourite CDs or tapes and have your own disco. Children can be encouraged to dance individually or work together to create a dance routine.

Create a marching band

Each child should have an instrument to play or be encouraged to clap their hands, stamp their feet or slap their thighs while marching.

Make your own instruments

Simple instruments such as maracas and drums can easily be made by filling plastic bottles with lentils, dried peas or pebbles (maracas) or using pans and wooden spoons (drums).

Teach children to learn about syllables

Introduce a game whereby the children have to clap out the beats in their name such as Sam-u-el or Da-vid.

Play a game of musical statues

Children should be encouraged to dance when they hear the music playing and, once the music stops, they need to stand still like 'statues'. The last person still dancing when the music stops is out.

Figure 10.6 Ideas for music activities

Role Play and Imaginative Play

Role play and imaginative play are all about 'make-believe'. Children will find inspiration from many things such as television, stories or real life events, all of which will provide them with the opportunity to act out their favourite scenes. The magic of the dressing-up box often proves irresistible to young children and a box of hats, belts, scarves, dresses and jewellery will open up a child's imagination. You can encourage children to explore different role play settings and to practise the rules of social behaviour by creating settings for them to act out their parts, such as providing a space in your setting for the children to:

- Visit the doctor
- Visit the dentist
- Take their dog to the vet

- Teach in a class room
- Eat in a café
- Go shopping
- Visit the hairdresser
- Catch an aeroplane to go on holiday.

Children will need very few props to act out these types of scenes; their imagination is usually all that is needed for them to play spontaneously in this way. Although children can take part in role play alone, it is frequently a social activity which is an excellent way of developing a child's communication skills.

Incorporating ICT

ICT can be incorporated very successfully in many areas of creative activities and computer programs which encourage children to draw can be fun and entertaining, encouraging the child to develop their own ideas and express themselves. Music is perhaps the activity which can incorporate technology more successfully than other areas. CD players, radios, cassettes, television, karaoke machines etc., all make music readily available. Instruments such as keyboards, synthesizers and electric guitars are all excellent ways of making different sounds and exploring music.

Overhead projectors and light boxes can help children to discover and create patterns and colour and paint programs encourage children to experiment with colour and different tools.

Useful Websites

www.activityvillage.co.uk

   Ideas for craft and activities for all ages

www.bakerross.co.uk

   Arts and craft materials

www.home-education.org.uk/scrap.htm

   Help locating your nearest recycling store for free materials

www.jollylearning.co.uk

   Songs and actions

www.magic-factory.co.uk

   An activity website offering online games which use colour and light

www.leapfroguk.com

   High-tech toys

www.onestopeducation.co.uk

   Music software

www.scholastic.co.uk

www.ss-services.co.uk

   Art and craft materials

www.2.sherston.com

   Set of ICT tools including writing and painting

How to Encourage Respect and Values in Children

11

Helping Children to Understand Social Acceptance

Children copy and learn from the adults around them. It is therefore important for adults to be good role models and to have high personal standards in order for children to do the same. Unfortunately this is not always the case and some adults teach negative attitudes by using bad language and showing aggression, prejudice and other forms of unacceptable behaviour.

Social acceptance is all about learning how to act in the company of others, how to build relationships, make friends and become accepted. In order to become socially accepted children need to learn who they are. They need to feel loved, valued and respected by those around them in order that they can begin to feel this way about others. It is important that child carers ensure that:

- The children in their care feel special. You need to encourage the children to feel loved, valued and respected by including everyone in the activities you provide and by listening to and valuing their thoughts, ideas and opinions.
- You provide a positive environment where all the children feel welcome and are allowed to learn and explore without the fear of failure or ridicule.
- You offer praise and encouragement.
- You have realistic expectations of what each child can achieve. This will depend on their age and stage of development. Never set targets which the children will find difficult to achieve as this can damage their confidence and self-esteem.

Remember

Children who experience love and respect are more likely to learn how to love and respect others.

Communicating with Adults

One of the most important things to remember, which probably sounds very obvious but is often overlooked, is that communication is a two-way process. Many people confuse talking *with* a child and talking *at* them. The two are very different. Talking *at* a child does not actually involve them in the communication and will not significantly promote their learning. Talking *with* a child is very different. It involves a meaningful, two-way conversation whereby the child and the adult share thoughts, views and ideas, and this method of communication effectively promotes learning.

Exercise

Can you be accused of talking *at* a child rather than *with* them on a regular basis? Take part in this simple exercise to see how many times you actually involve the child in your conversation.

Track your conversation with the child for 10 minutes and make note of:

- How many times you speak to the child.
- How many times the child speaks to you.
- Do you initiate the conversation or does the child?
- Do you give orders or suggestions?
- Do you listen to the child and share ideas?
- If the child asks a question do you answer it appropriately?
- If you ask a question do you allow the child sufficient time to answer it?

Although these questions may appear obvious, it is surprising how many adults lack the knowledge of how to communicate effectively with children. All too often adults spend little time talking to children unless they are barking orders at them or telling them off for acting inappropriately.

In order for a child to develop their own speech and vocabulary it is vital that they experience meaningful communication with both adults and other children. Adults are in a unique position to encourage children to speak slowly and clearly and to develop their speech effectively. You should be aiming to introduce new words every day and take the time to explain the meanings of any words that the child does not understand.

In addition to actual conversations, there are several other ways in which communication with adults can be both beneficial and educational to a child:

- Reading books and stories – sharing books and stories with children increases their language skills rapidly. Setting a good example yourself by reading slowly, using expression and speaking clearly will encourage the children to do the same. Books and stories are an excellent way of encouraging conversation and introducing new words. Extend the story time by discussing the tale together or try to guess the ending before you read it.
- Singing – sharing songs and action rhymes is another valuable learning activity for encouraging communication with adults.

Equal Opportunities

One of the basic requirements which all child carers need to show is that they will treat all children with equal concern. This does not mean treating all children the same, and this is where some people become confused with regard to equal opportunities. As child carers we do not treat all children the same. For example, you would not give a baby of six months old a knife and fork with which to eat their lunch, as you would a 6-year-old child. Nor would you expect the baby to be able to ride a bicycle or make a model with clay. Treating children with equal concern means allowing them the same opportunities to develop and learn regardless of their gender, culture, racial origins, family background or disability. It does not mean that we treat all children the same. All children should be seen as individuals and treated fairly and equally.

As a childcare practitioner you must be aware of how you can promote equal opportunities by treating all the children, and their parents and families, with equal concern. You must show respect to each family, their religion, beliefs and culture, and you must be confident when discouraging prejudice or dealing with stereotypical attitudes within your setting. It takes a strong person to stand up to prejudicial remarks and it may be worth considering how you would go about tackling any issues should they arise in your setting.

Exercise

Think about how you would respond to a parent who made a discriminatory remark about a child in your care. Would you ignore the comment or challenge the parent?

EQUAL OPPORTUNITIES POLICY

In order for all children and their families to feel valued and welcome in my setting I expect everyone to abide by a few simple rules.

Regardless of their racial origins, cultural or family background, gender, age or ability, all the children in my care will be:

Treated as individuals
Treated with equal concern
Given the opportunity to develop and learn

I will discourage any negative images, prejudice of any kind and stereotypical attitudes.

Figure 11.1 Example of an Equal Opportunities Policy

Although having an equal opportunities policy within your setting is not a guarantee that you will never come across prejudice, it does set the rules which you can reasonably expect parents to abide by whilst on your premises and, should you ever be confronted by a parent showing any form of prejudice, you can remind them of your policy.

Exercise

Make your own equal opportunities policy for your setting. Remember to take into account the wishes of the parents and ensure that your policy shows respect for different styles of parenting. Your policy should oppose all forms of discrimination and state that prejudicial behaviour will not be tolerated on your premises. The list below states some of the things you may like to consider when writing your equal opportunities policy:

- Religious issues
- Race issues

- Language issues
- Skin colour
- Gender
- Sexual orientation of the parents (lesbian mother, gay father)
- Marital status of the parents.

Disability

Every year babies in the United Kingdom are born with serious disabilities. These disabilities may include physical and sensory impairments, learning difficulties or medical conditions. Many childminders and nannies now choose to work with disabled children and their families and it is very important, if you choose to take on the responsibility of caring for a child with disabilities, that you understand their condition fully. You will need to work closely with the parents of the child and ensure that you know how to include the child in your daily routines and activities in order to understand, identify and break down any barriers involving the child's disability. It is your job to promote inclusion by treating all the children in your care as individuals and supporting their needs. It is an offence for any child carer to treat a child with a disability less favourably than any other child. It is paramount that you, as a child carer, understand that the needs of children with disabilities are the same as all children's needs. Avoid falling into the trap of providing activities for a child with a disability which do not effectively challenge them or allow them to express themselves freely, because this is deemed discriminatory. All children, regardless of any disability, need to play and should be provided with learning activities and resources appropriate to their age and stage of development. It may be necessary for you to adapt some of your toys and equipment to allow a child with a disability to take part such as positioning tables and trays so that they allow wheelchair access or providing cushions to support a child with mobility difficulties so that they can take part in activities along with the other children.

Prejudice and Discrimination

Despite legislation, many children and their families still suffer due to inequality and prejudice. As a childcare provider you should never exclude a child or their family from your setting because of differences in race, culture, religion, age or gender.

Discrimination and prejudice have a negative impact on children and their families, and giving people 'labels' takes away a person's identity and individuality.

> **Exercise**
>
> Consider the descriptions below.
>
> - Disabled, wheelchair user.
> - Football supporter.
> - Elderly gentleman.
> - Hell's Angel.
>
> What image do these descriptions portray to you? For example, do you see the football supporter as a hooligan or a family man enjoying his favourite sport with his children? Try to think of other descriptions whereby labelling someone may encourage negative assumptions.

Although discrimination is not always obvious or intentional, it is very important that child carers try, at all times, to avoid unintentionally ignoring the rights of others through lack of thought or by making negative assumptions. For example, a childminder may plan to make father's day cards with the children forgetting that not all the children may have contact with their father. It would have been better to suggest making cards for someone 'special' in the child's life, who may be their father, grandfather, uncle etc., in order to include everyone in the activity rather than just those who have access to their fathers.

A common misconception that children are unfortunately taught from an early age is that some toys and activities are more suited to boys than girls or vice versa. How many times have you witnessed a father saying that he doesn't want his son to dress up or play with a doll because he considers that 'girl's' play?

One of the most important and effective ways in which a child can learn is through watching, responding to and copying the reactions and behaviour of the people around them. Children will learn prejudice and form stereotypical attitudes if they experience them. Everyone has, and is entitled to, their own opinion; however, it is vital, when caring for children, that you do not impose your own views on them. Although you should not pretend that differences in people do not exist, you should be honest and open and encourage the children to be the same. Children need to learn that all people are unique and that differences in culture, religion and belief make each of us interesting.

Religion and Culture

Children who live in multicultural communities have frequent opportunities to learn from each other about the many traditions and festivals that form an important part of each different culture. However, some children who live in communities which are not multicultural may not be able to learn in this way and it then becomes more difficult for them to learn about the beliefs and traditions of others. This is where the role of the child carer comes in and, with careful planning, you should be able to introduce different cultures and traditions into your setting. This can be done in a variety of ways including:

- Introducing foods from different countries.
- Exploring different languages.
- Providing clothes and props for dressing up and role play.
- Teaching the children about different churches through the use of books and television.
- Using posters and wall displays.

Family Structures and How they Affect Children and Young People

Although it is very important, when you are caring for children from several families, that you make sure that everyone in the setting is aware of the policies and procedures you have, it is equally important to remember that just as every family is different so too are their values and views.

It is probably true to say that today's parents are heavily influenced by the way they themselves were brought up. Many of our values and beliefs will have come about as a result of what our own parents instilled in us as children and we are likely to echo the style of our parents when bringing up our own children.

In addition to the way we were brought up ourselves there are other influences which may affect the way in which we bring up our own children:

- Money and employment
- Housing
- Education
- Culture
- Family structure
- Religion.

It is probably true to say that parenting styles can be successfully divided into four main categories:

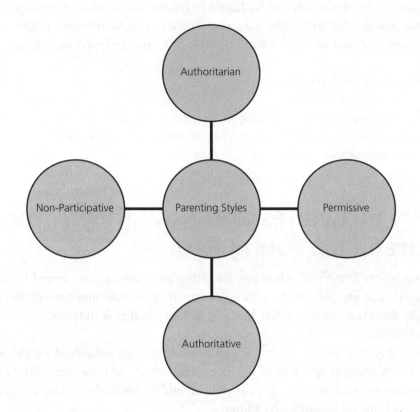

Figure 11.2 Parenting styles

Authoritarian

Authoritarian parents tend to be rather controlling and may have many rules which they expect their children to abide by. This type of parent may have high expectations of their children and there is a danger the child may find these expectations difficult to meet, which may result in the child feeling they have failed.

Permissive

Permissive parents are the opposite of authoritarian and often allow their children too much choice, resulting in children who are difficult to manage. The danger posed by permissive parents is that their children may be overwhelmed by such freedom of choice and become afraid of making the wrong decisions.

Authoritative

The majority of parents are authoritative. They attempt to shape their child's behaviour in a way that will enable them to become socially acceptable.

Non-Participative

This type of parent appears to reject their child, perhaps because of stress or illness. Non-participative parents are over-permissive and uncontrolling.

In addition to parenting styles, family structures also have an enormous effect on the way that children are brought up. There are six main types of family structures:

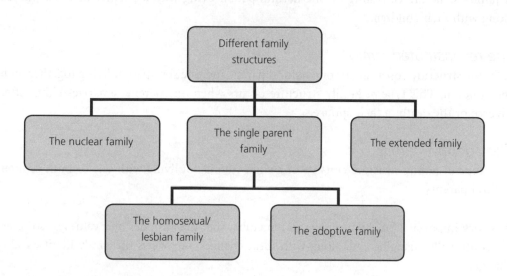

Figure 11.3 Family structures

The nuclear family

A family structure where both parents and their children live together and share the responsibility of caring for their children.

The single parent family

A family structure consisting of one parent living on their own with their children. This type of family structure may occur for several reasons:

- The child's parents may be separated or divorced.
- The child's mother may have decided to have a child without opting for a relationship with the father.
- One of the child's natural parents may have died.

The extended family

A family structure consisting of parents, children and relatives all living close by and sometimes even in the same house, sharing the responsibility of childcare. This kind of family structure was traditional in this country for centuries and is still common practice in many parts of the world.

The homosexual/lesbian family

A family structure consisting of one natural parent living with a partner of the same sex along with their children.

The reconstituted family

A family structure consisting of one natural parent and one step-parent living together with the children. This type of family structure occurs when one parent remarries either after divorce or the death of their spouse.

The adoptive family

This type of family structure consists of a child who is not living with one or both of their natural parents.

It is very important for childminders to remember that the attitudes and values of societies are continually changing and, along with these changes, our views on family life itself also change.

It could be argued that the number of 'traditional' families consisting of a married man and woman living with their children is on the decline. We know that the number of births outside marriage has increased. It is because of these changes that childminders should not make any assumptions and judgements regarding the type of family in which a child is living.

Although it is necessary, for the smooth running of a childminding business, to have certain rules and regulations, it is equally important to remember that parents and families may have different approaches to certain things when bringing up their children. While your own personal style of care will be what attracted the parents to you in the first place, you must respect any differences in values and principles.

It is important that childminders feel confident in their approach to certain issues regarding the care of children and you should have discussed important issues with the parents of the children before commencement of the contract. However, it is good business practice to remember that compromise is important and wherever possible you should try to accommodate parents wishes with regard to the care of their children.

Children may have different sets of rules to follow depending on whether they are at home, at the childminders, or at school, and it is important that they understand why certain rules are necessary and you must explain why these rules may differ from setting to setting. Everyone has the right to their own opinion and way of doing things and it is paramount that both adults and children are aware of these differences and are encouraged to respect and understand them.

A Look at Unacceptable Behaviour in Young Children

Personality plays an important part in the way a child behaves. It is important to understand the way a child's personality develops. Although there is no exact way of knowing if a child's inherited traits have more of an effect on the way they grow and develop than the influences of where they live and who they meet, it is probably true to say that many personal traits of the child are inherited from their parents.

Exercise

Think about your own personality and that of your parents. Would you describe yourself as being like one or neither of your parents? How many times have you heard someone liken you, your own children, or the children you care for, to their parents? How many times have you yourself said 'She's really shy and quiet, just like her father' or 'He's really outgoing and confident, must get that from his mother'?

It is probably true to say that there is no real way of knowing how certain problems and pressures affecting parents today will influence their children over time. However, it may be argued that some of the factors involved affect the way in which children behave. For example, separation and divorce may make a child feel unloved and abandoned, whereas the birth of a new baby could bring out feelings of jealousy and resentment.

The way in which children see themselves will have an enormous effect on their behaviour. Children need to feel that they 'belong'. There are three essential elements to a child's self-esteem:

- Self worth: children have a need to feel significant. They want to be accepted, loved and respected by those around them. A child who feels worthless and unwanted will develop low self-esteem. Children need to feel good about themselves.
- Control: children very quickly learn how to control situations and they will learn that when they behave in a certain way their actions can bring about changes. For example, a tantrum may result in the child getting his or her own way, and a crying baby will demand his or her mother's attention. Self-esteem is directly affected by the amount of control a child has over a particular situation.
- Competence: a child who feels competent and capable will be encouraged to learn new skills and develop motivation. It is important that our expectations of children are realistic in order for them to develop competence and limit failure.

There are many factors in a child's life which will influence the way in which they behave and it is important that we are aware of and understand these factors if we are to understand the child's behaviour.

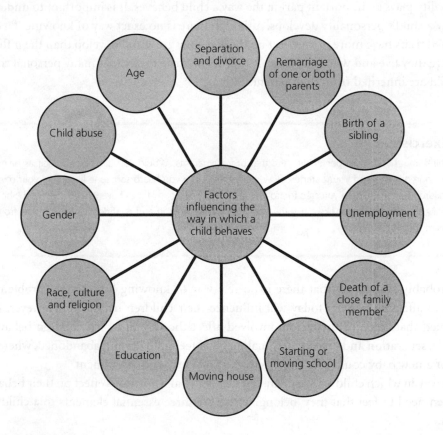

Figure 11.4 Factors influencing how children behave

Any one or more of the above factors may influence the way in which a child behaves.

The figure below gives examples of some of the feelings a child may experience which may result in unwanted behaviour.

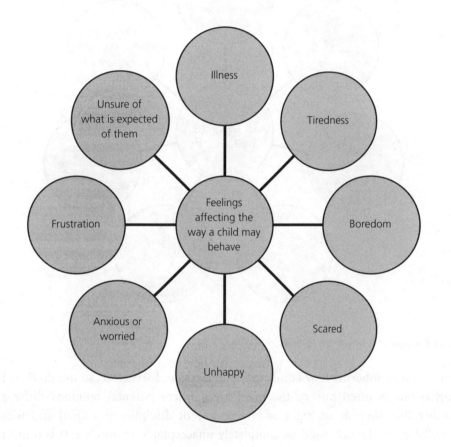

Figure 11.5 Feelings affecting how children behave

Children may also show signs of unacceptable behaviour if

- They have a particular learning difficulty, allergy etc.
- They do not have clear, consistent boundaries to follow.

It may sometimes feel as though a child is purposely refusing to cooperate. However, it is important to remember that all children will act up from time to time, but there may also be other reasons for their behaviour such as:

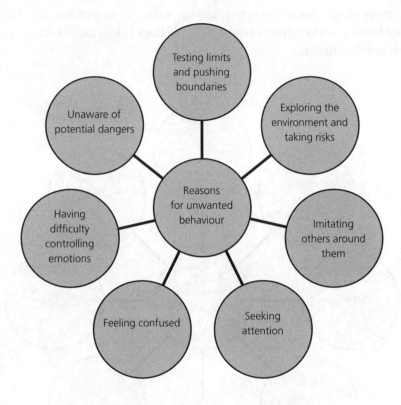

Figure 11.6 Reasons for unwanted behaviour

Once again, remembering how families differ in style and structure, so too do their beliefs, and behaviour is often one of the main areas where parental opinions differ greatly. Remember that there is no right or wrong way of disciplining a child and what may work well for one family could be completely unacceptable in another. It is important to understand what constitutes unacceptable behaviour and why.

Unacceptable behaviour is when a child:

- Resorts to tantrums
- Bites, screams or lashes out
- Spoils the games of others
- Swears and becomes rude and offensive
- Becomes oppositional
- Becomes demanding
- Becomes destructive
- Tells lies.

The reasons why this behaviour is unacceptable is because it will make the child unwelcome or unacceptable to others, result in danger to either the child themselves or to others, appear hurtful or offensive, or damage property.

Encouraging Acceptable Behaviour in Young Children

Most children want to behave in a way which is appropriate and acceptable and they usually want to please the adults around them. While it is probably true to say that all children will display some form of unacceptable behaviour from time to time, it is also true that only a minority of children will display the kind of behaviour which causes concern.

As a childminder it is essential that you are aware of how to manage unwanted behaviour, however it is equally important that you are aware of how to encourage and promote positive behaviour.

Exercise

Think about how you would react if you were caring for two children, one of whom was sitting quietly reading a book while the other was pulling the books off the shelf and scattering them on the floor. To which child would you give the most attention? Why would you give this child more attention than the other?

There are many different strategies for encouraging and guiding children to manage their own behaviour and it is important that childcare practitioners are aware of these strategies and know how to try a different approach if one particular strategy appears to be ineffective.

Strategies

The following are some successful strategies for managing children's behaviour:

Empowerment
This is when a child is given the opportunity to be in control of a situation and to work things out for themselves. We can help a child to feel empowered by developing their confidence and self-esteem in a way that encourages them to manage their own behaviour.

In order to empower a child we must listen carefully to what they are telling us so that we can be certain we know exactly what they need and want.

Providing children with simple tasks and choices, suitable to their age and level of understanding also helps a child to feel empowered.

Acknowledging the way a child feels

A child's feelings can be very strong and, at times, difficult for them to control. They may experience both positive and negative feelings including excitement, anger and fear and it is very important that childminders respect and acknowledge these feelings. It is vital that we do not dismiss a child's feelings but instead encourage the child to express them and learn how to deal with them.

Setting clear and consistent boundaries

A child can often display unwanted behaviour if they are unsure of what is expected of them. It is unfair of us to expect a child to behave in a certain way if the goals and boundaries we set are inconsistent and confusing. When deciding on a framework for setting limits and boundaries it is important to take into account the feelings of the child and your main concerns should be:

- The child's safety
- The child's well-being
- The child's overall development.

It is important that any rules and boundaries you set are appropriate to the age and development of the children in your care, and you must ask yourself the following questions:

- Are your rules fair?
- Are your rules easy to understand?
- Is the child aware of the consequences of breaking these rules?

Exercise

Think about the way you react to situations. If things were not going according to plan, for example if you couldn't find your keys or if a child spills a drink, how would you react? Would you fly off the handle, rush around feeling harassed and stressed, or would you sort the problem in a calm, relaxed manner?

Providing the child with a positive role model

A role model who is aggressive and abusive will not set a good example to a child and the chances are the child will copy this kind of behaviour. We are all guilty of being angry, upset, confused and annoyed some of the time but it is important, when in the company of young children, to think about our actions and control our feelings of temper in order to set children a good example. Show children how you cope in adverse situations and teach them how to control their anger and overcome their emotions.

Guiding the child

By continually talking to the children in your care you will be guiding them and helping them to succeed. Simple tasks such as setting the table can be broken up into small achievable steps which will enable the child to carry out successfully what is expected of them. For example, you could guide a child to do this task by:

- Encouraging them to count how many people will be sitting down to eat.
- Helping them to count out the correct number of knives, forks and spoons.
- Showing them how to position the cutlery correctly on the table.

By guiding the child you will have effectively helped them to achieve their goal and boosted their self-confidence and self-esteem.

Offering praise and encouragement

It is not always easy to get a child to behave in a certain way and many young children can be stubborn and uncooperative. However, by focusing on the positive things and rewarding the good behaviour you will go a long way to encouraging children to behave appropriately. All too often adults forget to respond to acceptable behaviour and overlook a child who is playing well. It is important to remember that sometimes a child's need for attention is greater than their fear of being reprimanded and they will resort to unwanted behaviour simply to receive the desired effect. In a child's eyes negative attention is often seen as being preferable to no attention at all. Try ignoring inappropriate behaviour and focusing on the children who are displaying good behaviour. It is important that you praise and reward good behaviour and never overlook it.

Using positive language and giving children choices will go a long way to reinforcing good behaviour. Avoid using negative statements or commands and instead try making suggestions and offering alternatives.

> **Exercise**
> Take note of the conversations you have with the children over the next 30 minutes. How many times do you 'tell' the children to do something rather than 'ask or request' them to do it? What kind of response do you get from the children if you ask rather than command?

Positive behaviour in children can be promoted in several ways:

- Encouraging children to understand about behaviour and what is considered appropriate.
- Setting clear, consistent boundaries which the children can understand.
- Praising good behaviour.
- Ignoring unacceptable behaviour.
- Using rewards.
- Allowing the children freedom of choice when appropriate.
- Allowing the children the opportunity to be in control of situations when appropriate.

Using rewards

Rewards can be very effective when promoting positive behaviour in children; however, it is important that they are not mistaken for bribery. Many adults would raise the question of whether it is ethical to encourage a child to behave well in return for a reward. However, providing rewards are used sparingly and encourage a child to put in more effort with regard to behaviour management, I see no reason why they shouldn't be used. After all, rewards or privileges have been earned if a child has shown exceptional behaviour.

Rewarding a child who has shown good behaviour and who has tried hard encourages self-esteem and confidence. Rewards may take the form of:

- Verbal praise
- Smiles
- Hugs
- Stickers
- Smiley faces
- Stars
- Toys
- Sweets
- Fruit
- Choosing next activity
- Certificates.

Rewards should always be offered to a child immediately after they have shown good behaviour in order to reinforce what has been achieved. Giving a child a reward or praising them for something that they have done well after the event will be ineffective as they may have forgotten what they did to warrant the reward. Always reward good behaviour immediately. Rewards should be given often at the outset and then, when a child finds a particular task easier, the reward can be given less frequently. The impact of the reward will be lost on a child who can perform a particular task easily; in order for the child to remain motivated the task should be challenging.

Rewards

Small toys of gifts

A reward of a small toy or gift should not be used regularly because you risk the child behaving well only to achieve a present rather than because they actually want to display good behaviour. Toys and gifts should be kept to a minimum but could be used in exceptional circumstances, for example if the child has experienced the birth of a new sibling and coped admirably with the addition to their family without resorting to jealousy, or if the child has had to cope with a particularly stressful time such as starting school or playgroup.

Choosing the next activity

This is an excellent way of praising a child and will boost their confidence and self-esteem. A child who has behaved well and shown understanding and caring could be rewarded with a choice of activities.

Individual attention

Often just a few minutes of your undivided attention can boost a child's confidence and self-esteem immeasurably. Take the time to ask the child questions and, more importantly, to listen to what they have to tell you. Giving a child individual attention when they have behaved well will eliminate the need for them to misbehave in order to be noticed.

Stickers

Stickers are often used in the nursery and school setting to reward effort and exceptional behaviour. Verbal praise can be followed up with the use of stickers to reaffirm the child's behaviour and give them something tangible to show to their parents and friends.

Sweets and fruit

Sweets should always be used in moderation, and only with the permission of the child's parents, to reward a child's positive behaviour. Fruit, raisins, celery sticks etc., are a healthier alternative and can be offered as a reward for good behaviour.

Reward charts

Charts are often used in conjunction with other rewards as a way of monitoring and recording a child's behaviour. If a child receives a reward for good behaviour it is a good idea to follow this up with a recognition next to their name on your reward chart. Stars, stickers or smiley faces can be used next to a child's name on a reward chart and after a set period of time, perhaps a week or a month, the stars, stickers or smiley faces can be tallied up to see who has achieved the most. A small gift may then be given to the child who has gained the most rewards on the chart. A reward chart may look something like this:

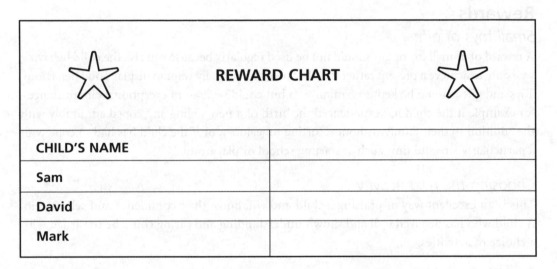

Figure 11.7 Example of a reward chart

A special certificate could be given to the child who has achieved the most rewards at the end of a set period of time.

A certificate could be completed to include what the child has done to achieve it or could be pre-printed to look something like this:

THIS

CERTIFICATE

HAS BEEN AWARDED TO

....

FOR SHOWING SPECIAL BEHAVIOUR THIS WEEK

HE/SHE HAS BEEN:

KIND

CONSIDERATE

HELPFUL

POLITE

WELL DONE!

Figure 11.8 Example of a certificate for good behaviour

Children should be praised and rewarded when they have shown pleasing behaviour, such as:

- Taking turns
- Sharing
- Being friendly
- Being sensible
- Being patient
- Being brave
- Showing kindness to others
- Helping to tidy up
- Having a good idea

- Giving a good answer
- Being thoughtful
- Helping others
- Asking a thought-provoking question
- Showing self-help skills such as putting on their own coat or shoes.

Children often become over-excited and boisterous, which can result in noisy and unwanted behaviour. It can sometimes be difficult for excited children to calm down, especially if they are looking forward to a particular event such as Christmas or a birthday or if they have been playing outdoors and letting off steam. A good way of getting children to lower the volume indoors in a positive way is to introduce a 'noise chart' into your setting. Such a chart will encourage the children to refrain from being too loud hopefully without the need for the childminder to reprimand the children verbally. A noise chart may look something like this:

TOO NOISY	An arrow should be used positioned at the appropriate level of volume so that children can clearly see if they are being too noisy.
STILL TOO LOUD	
JUST THE RIGHT VOLUME	

Figure 11.9 Example of a noise chart

Responding to Unacceptable Behaviour

Whatever strategy you use and however successful your reward system, there is one thing for sure, the children you care for will resort to unwanted behaviour at some point. No child behaves well all the time; moreover, a child who never puts a foot wrong or never tests the boundaries will probably cause you more concern than a child who occasionally misbehaves.

It is how you respond to a child's unacceptable behaviour that will prove whether or not your behaviour management is successful.

It is important when faced with a child who is misbehaving to:

- Ensure that you remain calm and in control of the situation.
- Never resort to shouting, losing your temper or using physical punishment.

> **Remember**
>
> When you lose control of the situation the child has effectively won. By allowing yourself to become angry and to shout or lash out you have lost the ability to control the situation. You will be giving out the wrong signals to the child, effectively giving out the message that losing control and shouting is acceptable behaviour when in fact it is exactly the type of behaviour you are hoping to avoid.

It is very important when managing children's behaviour that you follow a few simple rules in order that everyone understands exactly what is expected of them.

> **Effective steps to promote positive behaviour in children**
>
> Be consistent and mean what you say.
> Use praise and rewards when appropriate.
> Ignore unwanted behaviour.
> Ensure you are a good role model at all times.
> Apply sanctions when necessary.

Figure 11.10 Promoting positive behaviour

> **Exercise**
>
> Think carefully about the way you personally handle situations where a child has shown unacceptable behaviour. When you say 'no' to a child do you mean it or do you allow the child to 'win you over', thus giving in to their demands?

> **Exercise**
>
> Imagine that you are caring for two children aged 2 and 3 years. The 2-year-old is on the verge of resorting to a tantrum because he wants the toy car that the 3-year-old is playing with. How would you deal with this situation?

Behaviour in Older Children

As children get older the way they behave changes. They may no longer resort to tantrums, for example, if they can't get their own way. However, they may well learn other undesirable traits. Unacceptable behaviour in older children may take the form of:

- Swearing
- Telling lies
- Manipulation
- Bullying.

As children continue to grow and develop they need adults around them who can support their needs, adults who know when to intervene and when to take a step back. Part of growing up is about learning from our mistakes and children should be allowed the freedom to make choices and accept the consequences of their behaviour. Adults need to be on hand to praise their efforts and good behaviour and allow them to become independent. As children move through school they will experience many changes in routines and make new relationships. Adults need to be sensitive to these changes and be aware of the decisions that young people face.

Children between 13 and 16 years of age often begin to rebel and may resort to truanting and disruption. The need to be accepted by their friends and peers is paramount and may cause conflict with parents and carers. Depression and anxiety are widely experienced by young people of this age and, as parents and carers, it is vital that we remain non-judgemental but alert to any major changes in their moods.

Useful Websites

www.kidscape.org.uk
   Kidscape: preventing bulling and child abuse
www.bullying.co.uk
   Bullying Online: help and advice on bullying
www.childline.org.uk
   Helpline for children and young people

Promoting Safe Play

Child Rights and Protection

The United Nations Convention on the Rights of the Child (UNCRC) was drawn up in 1989. There are 54 articles contained within the UNCRC of which 5 primarily affect childcare practitioners:

Article 2   Children have a right to be protected from all forms of discrimination.

Article 3   The best interests of the child must be the primary consideration in all activities and actions concerning the child.

Article 12   Children have a right to express their views freely. Their views will be given appropriate consideration in accordance with their age and maturity.

Article 13   Children have the right to freedom of expression and the exchange of information.

Article 28   Children have a right to education.

Essentially the UNCRC states that all children must be shown respect and their interests must be treated with importance. The UNCRC is designed to protect the rights of children and young people under the age of 18 years. The following chart outlines the various pieces of legislation pertaining to children and explains their focus.

Education Act 1981	Recognition of: • parents' rights with regard to their child's education • special educational needs.
United Nations Convention on the Rights of the Child 1989	An agreement by many nations stating that all children should have the right to specific things such as: • a right to education • a right to shelter • a right to food.
Children Act 1989	This act was the United Kingdom's first official acknowledgement in UK law of the rights of children. The emphasis of this act was that the 'needs of the child are paramount'.
Education Act 1987	This act set a time frame on the legal process of identifying and assessing children's needs.
Data Protection Act 1998	In the case of children, this act made it necessary for consent to be given by the parents before any confidential or personal information about the child is passed on.
National Standards for Under Eights Day Care and Childminding 2001	This legislation made is necessary for all early years childcare practitioners to meet a set of standards. The standards for England are monitored by Ofsted. The standards for Wales are monitored by the Care Standards Inspectorate for Wales. The standards for Scotland are monitored by the Scottish Care Commission; and the standards for Northern Ireland are monitored by the local Health and Social Services Trust.
Birth to Three Matters – a Framework for Effective Practice 2002	Although this framework is not legislation, it has been put in place to support, inform, guide

	and challenge practitioners working in the early years sector.
Children Act 2004	This act came about from the Green Paper 'Every Child Matters' and relates to five specific outcomes for all children: • be healthy • stay safe • enjoy and achieve • make a positive contribution • achieve economic well-being.
Children Act 2006	This Act placed a duty on all local authorities to provide sufficient childcare to meet the needs of all families. The Act also requires the development of the Early Years Foundation Stage, a framework to support the delivery of integrated care and education for babies and children under the age of 5.

Figure 12.1 Children's legislation

Health and Safety

As part of the registration process your childminding setting will be checked for cleanliness and safety. It is very important that your standards are high at all times and that you set good examples for the children in your care. Children learn from copying those around them and you can encourage good hygiene practices by ensuring that you always wash your hands after visiting the toilet and that you cover your mouth when coughing and sneezing in order to prevent the spread of infection.

> **Remember**
>
> It is an offence for anyone to smoke on the premises while children are being cared for. This includes the parents of the children and your partner/spouse.

You have a responsibility for the safety and well-being at all times of the children in your care. The most important and effective way of ensuring this safety when the children are playing or enjoying activities is through constant supervision and by following certain steps to prevent accidents:

- ## Supervision

  This is the single most effective way of ensuring the children are safe and it means that you are aware of what *all* of the children are doing *all* of the time. You must be able to see and/or hear them at all times and this includes while they are playing both indoors and out.

- ## Toy Safety Standards

  As part of the Consumer Protection Act 2002, a European Directive was introduced into British law by the Toys Safety Regulations 1995. To ensure the safety of the toys you purchase, always look for the logo of the British Toy and Hobby Association which indicates that the toys meet satisfactory safety standards. This logo is widely known as the 'Lion Mark'. Other safety symbols include the letters (CE). Toys bearing this symbol meet the European standards. Despite these standards being introduced, it is unfortunately still possible for illegal and potentially dangerous toys to be purchased in this country and you should be extra vigilant when purchasing toys and equipment from jumble sales and market stalls.

- ## Battery operated toys

  Batteries are usually considered as a safe source of power provided they are used correctly. Batteries should be:

  - fitted correctly into the toy
  - covered once fitted
  - disposed of correctly when spent and never burned
  - of an appropriate size for the age of the children (small mercury disc batteries, for example, should never be used when caring for young children as they pose a danger if swallowed or inserted in the ears or nose).

- ## Toys with small pieces

  Toys which include small pieces or which are designed for older children should never be in reach of younger children and you should think carefully about how and where these are to be stored when not in use.

- ## Broken toys

  Any toy which is broken or has a missing piece should be removed so that the children cannot get hold of it. You must then decide whether the toy can be safely repaired or the missing part replaced. If you are in any doubt about the safety of the toy you should throw it away immediately.

- **Regular checks**

  It is good practice to check your toys and equipment on a regular basis for wear and tear, broken and missing parts. A written record is a good way of logging the date the checks were made and it is a good idea to replace batteries during these checks. It is far better to be vigilant and to have good safety standards than to have to deal with an accident.

- **Outdoor toys and equipment**

  It is all too easy to forget about the toys and equipment you have outdoors, particularly in the winter months when perhaps they are not used as often. However it is vital that you make regular checks to ensure that any climbing frames, swings etc., are set up correctly and securely fastened to the ground. Check for rust and corrosion, particularly after a long period of inactivity during the winter months. Sand-pits should be covered when not in use and ride-on toys should be regularly checked for broken or missing parts.

Exercise

Make your own toy safety plan. Incorporate toys which need regular checking for wear and tear, batteries etc. Include the dates the checks were made and what action was taken.

Dangers Online

All schools now have computers. Many children also have access to a computer at home and it is therefore important that children become familiar with them and learn to use them with ease. Email and the internet are becoming an increasingly common method of communication and can open up a whole new world of learning for children – provided they are used correctly. Although computers can be both entertaining and educational it is necessary to supervise children when they are online as the internet is also a useful tool for people wishing to exploit children.

Recent cases in the news have highlighted how internet chat rooms can be used by paedophiles who make relationships with children by 'grooming' them to become victims either over the internet itself or by arranging to meet them in person. Children become victims without realizing it by wrongly believing they are chatting to other children because they cannot see who they are talking to when using these chat rooms.

The internet also poses a real danger to children with regard to pornography. Pornographic images of children are, sadly, in high demand and there is a great risk from people who take sexual pictures of children, to get young children involved over the internet.

Despite the dangers of the internet it is still a useful tool when used correctly and there are ways in which you can help to protect children while they are online which will ensure that the time they spend 'logged on' will be safe, fun and informative:

- Always supervise children while they are on the internet.
- Ask your Internet Service Provider about parental controls which prevent children from accessing websites with sexual or other harmful content.
- Learn about the internet. By being aware of the dangers yourself you can warn children and lay down certain ground rules to safeguard them while they are on the internet, for example the length of time they are allowed to log on for and which sites they can visit.
- Be aware of the possible signs of exploitation. In particular take note of any new friendships between the child and older people, both male and female, and be aware of any changes in the child's mood or the way they act.

Television

Television programmes, videos and DVDs which children are allowed to view can have an enormous impact on a child's disposition. Common sense tells us that children who regularly have access to violent viewing material may well become aggressive. Children like to copy the things they see and will imitate the violent scenes they view. The 'watershed' is in place to protect young children from unsuitable viewing material before 9pm but often, hours before this time, violent scenes can be witnessed on programmes supposedly aimed at family viewing.

News bulletins can be particularly traumatising for young children as world tragedies and disasters are reported on a daily basis. Adults who understand what is going on can communicate with one another and talk through their feelings and opinions on newsworthy topics. Children, on the other hand, often lack the skills to communicate their feelings and are therefore coping silently with what they have seen. Very young children may lack the vocabulary to express their anxieties and concerns and although news headlines may well upset them, they may resort to expressing their fears in a non-verbal way, such as re-enacting what they have seen, rather than discussing the events.

It is probably true to say that most parents are aware of the unsuitable nature of certain films, videos and DVDs and prevent their children from viewing this type of material. However, they often completely forget about the very graphic scenes portrayed on the news bulletins several times a day. Whereas it is probably true to say that some children find it difficult to distinguish between fantasy and reality and may well think the news is just another 'pretend' programme, others may be disturbed by the suffering they witness on screen. War and other world tragedies such as the Asian Tsunami, the Twin Towers and the London bombings were broadcast over and over again and there is a real possibility of young children thinking the scale of the tragedy is even greater because of the repetitive media coverage.

Playing with Guns and Other Toy Weapons

It has been discussed time and time again whether or not it is appropriate for childcare professionals to allow young children to play with toy guns and weapons. Our instincts tell us that we should not be encouraging children to play at make-believe shooting and stabbing. It is widely believed that children who play aggressively with guns and other toy weapons are more likely to be aggressive with their friends. Although this may not be completely true, it is disturbing to watch young children pretend to kill or injure one another. Is it possible or indeed necessary, then, for us to ban completely toy weapons of any sort in the playroom? Children have pretended to be cops and robbers, pirates and cowboys for years and many adults feel that there is no harm in children enjoying these types of games. What is important is that we should not simply focus on the toys a child is allowed to use but more importantly on the other influences which may affect a child's behaviour and result in aggression.

There are many influences on children's aggression such as:

- Their upbringing – are their parents aggressive by nature? Do they deal with conflict in an appropriate, managed way or angrily?
- Television – are the children exposed to violent films or programmes? Even cartoons aimed at children can be extremely violent.
- DVDs – even if children are not allowed to watch television after the 9pm watershed they may still be exposed to unsuitable violent films through DVDs and videos.

It is important to remember that, even if you do ban toy guns and other weapons in your childminding setting, children may well create their own! How many times have the children in your setting made a toy gun in the garden from a stick or a pretend sword using cardboard? Avoid banning toy guns and other toy weapons because, apart from encouraging the children to make their own, it may even enhance their interest if they realize that toy weapons are 'off limits'. It is not possible to stifle all kinds of 'aggressive' play and in fact trying to do so may well hinder the child's development and make them even more disruptive. Children need an outlet to release their innate aggression and this should be encouraged through play.

> **Exercise**
> How would you allow children to release innate aggression and pent-up energy in the childminding setting without the use of toy weapons?

It is probably true to say that the way around the toy weapon debate is to avoid implementing a total ban on these toys. Relaxed attitudes towards toy weapons will allow the children to explore without restriction. It is entirely up to you, of course, whether you decide to allow children to play with toy weapons in your setting and your own approach to these toys may well differ from that of others. Things to bear in mind when deciding which, if any, toy weapons you will allow the children to play with in your setting:

- Allow the children the opportunity to release their aggression and energy by supervising 'pretend-fighting'. Under supervision this type of play is harmless. Pretend fighting should be allowed *occasionally* and not dominate the day's activities.
- Encourage children to view 'super heroes' in a new light. They need not always be powerful, weapon-wielding men fighting off enemies. Give children the message that super heroes can be caring as well as strong.
- Talk to the children about any concerns you may have. Explain to them that you don't like to see them appearing aggressive and fighting and point out that real guns and weapons hurt and kill people and are very dangerous. Often young children have no idea of the concept of weapons, what they are really used for, and how deadly they can be.
- Do not discourage the children from making their own toy weapons. Building bricks such as Lego are ideal for constructing toy guns and weapons because these bricks can be weapons one minute and a tower block, car or robot the next, depending entirely on the play concept the child has in mind.
- If you do decide to buy toy guns and weapons for the children to play with, then it is best if you avoid purchasing items which look much like the real thing. Guns and swords which are replicas of the real thing may well stimulate a child's fascination.
- Choose your television viewing carefully and supervise everything the children are allowed to watch. Avoid aggressive cartoons and violent news programmes while the children are in your setting.

Bullying

The definition of a bully is an adult or child who deliberately intimidates of persecutes someone with the intention of causing them distress.

Bullying can be either physical, social, psychological or verbal, and take the form of:

- Physical attacks – hitting, kicking, punching, damaging of property.
- Threat of physical attacks - intimidation.
- Social attacks – racial abuse or remarks, exclusion.
- Psychological attacks – torment or ridicule.
- Verbal attacks – name calling, spreading of gossip or rumours, sarcasm.

As a childcare practitioner you have a responsibility to the children in your care and if you have reason to believe that a child you are looking after is either being bullied or in fact bullying someone themselves, then it is paramount that you act. Never ignore a disclosure from a child of abuse.

Although it is often thought that the victims of bullying are the only ones in need of sympathy and support, it is true to say that the bullies themselves need help and guidance. People bully for a number of reasons:

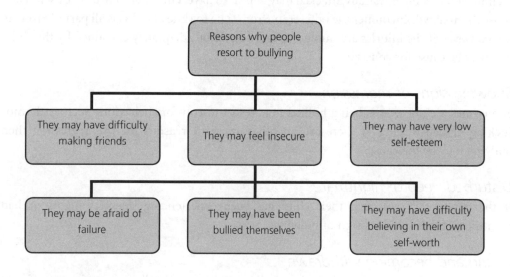

Figure 12.2 Reasons why people bully

In order to prevent a child from resorting to bullying it is important that you understand the problems and issues they may be facing.

Bullies are often angry and aggressive and you will need to work closely with the child, their parents and, if necessary, the child's school in order to work out a suitable strategy for dealing with any issues of bullying.

Many victims of bullying try to hide their feelings and it is not always easy to recognize when a child is being bullied. One of the most important things you should be aware of are any major changes to a child's usual disposition as this can often be an early warning sign for a child who is being bullied. Changes in a child's behaviour which may be a result of bullying are many and varied, but you should always take notice if a child in your care exhibits any of the following signs.

Refusal to go to school

Often a child who is being bullied at school will look for reasons to avoid being in contact with the person who is causing them distress. They may fake illness, complaining of tummy ache or headache in the hope that they can avoid having to go to school. If this kind of behaviour is unusual for the child in question then you should be wary of the reasons.

Unexplained injuries and ripped clothing

A child who is being physically attacked may appear to have a number of bruises or scratches. Most children will encounter the odd scrape from time to time and this is all part of growing up. However, if the injuries are numerous and cannot be adequately explained by the child, this may be cause for concern.

Showing signs of regression

Sometimes a child who is being bullied may resort to comfort behaviour such as thumb-sucking or bed-wetting. If there are no other apparent reasons for this regression then bullying may be the cause.

Disturbed sleep or nightmares

If the parent tells you that their child has been experiencing sleepless nights or bad nightmares this could be a sign of bullying.

Crying and becoming withdrawn

Victims of bullying often try to hide their feelings and refuse to tell anyone of their suffering in case they face repercussions. A child who is usually outgoing and happy but who suddenly becomes withdrawn and upset may be cause for concern.

Other factors such as being physically sick, attempting to self harm or a deterioration in school work may also be signs that a child is being bullied. The single most important factor to look out for is a substantial change in the child's usual behaviour.

Exercise

A child in your care has told you that they don't want to go to school because they are being bullied by others in their class. Write down the procedure you would follow to solve this problem.

Bullying Policies

Bullying can have far-reaching repercussions and affect a child indefinitely. It is a very serious issue which can vary considerably in severity and the response it provokes. You can encourage children to be aware of bullying and how it affects people by drawing their attention to the type of behaviour which is unacceptable. Introducing a bullying policy into your setting can help to outline the type of behaviour you are not willing to tolerate and, hopefully, encourage children to be more tolerant of others.

BULLYING POLICY

Bullying can have far-reaching effects on people

and causes unnecessary hurt and distress.

In order for everyone to feel welcome and valued within

my setting I will NOT tolerate:

* Name calling and verbal abuse
* Fighting
* Physical attacks of any kind
* Threatening behaviour
* Racial or disciminatory remarks
* Exclusion of one child by another

Figure 12.3 Example of a bullying policy

Useful Websites

www.capt.org.uk
  Child Accident Prevention Trust
www.childminding.org
  Scottish Childminding Association
www.ncma.org.uk
  National Childminding Association
www.nicma.org
  Northern Ireland Childminding Association
www.nspcc.org.uk
  The National Society for the Prevention of Cruelty to Children
www.rights4me.org.uk
www.rospa.com
  Royal Society for the Prevention of Accidents

Index